Cram101 Textbook Outlines to accompany:

Later Life: The Realities of Aging

Cox, 6th Edition

An Academic Internet Publishers (AIPI) publication (c) 2007.

You have a discounted membership at www.Cram101.com with this book.

Get all of the practice tests for the chapters of this textbook, and access in-depth reference material for writing essays and papers. Here is an example from a Cram101 Biology text:

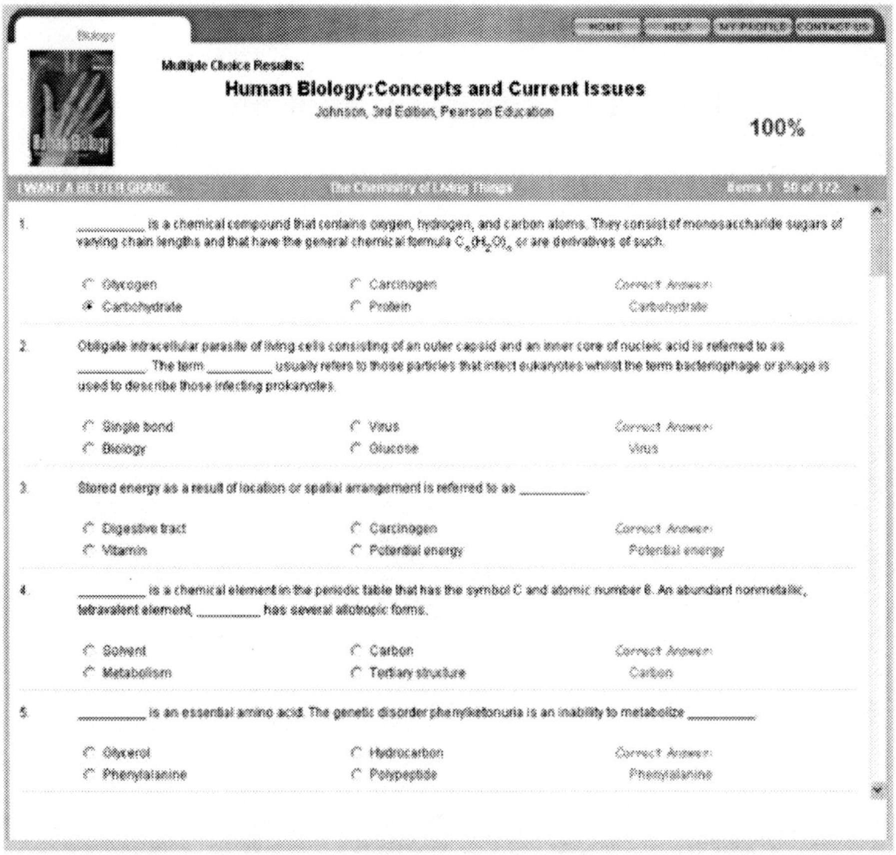

When you need problem solving help with math, stats, and other disciplines, www.Cram101.com will walk through the formulas and solutions step by step.

With Cram101.com online, you also have access to extensive reference material.

You will nail those essays and papers. Here is an example from a Cram101 Biology text:

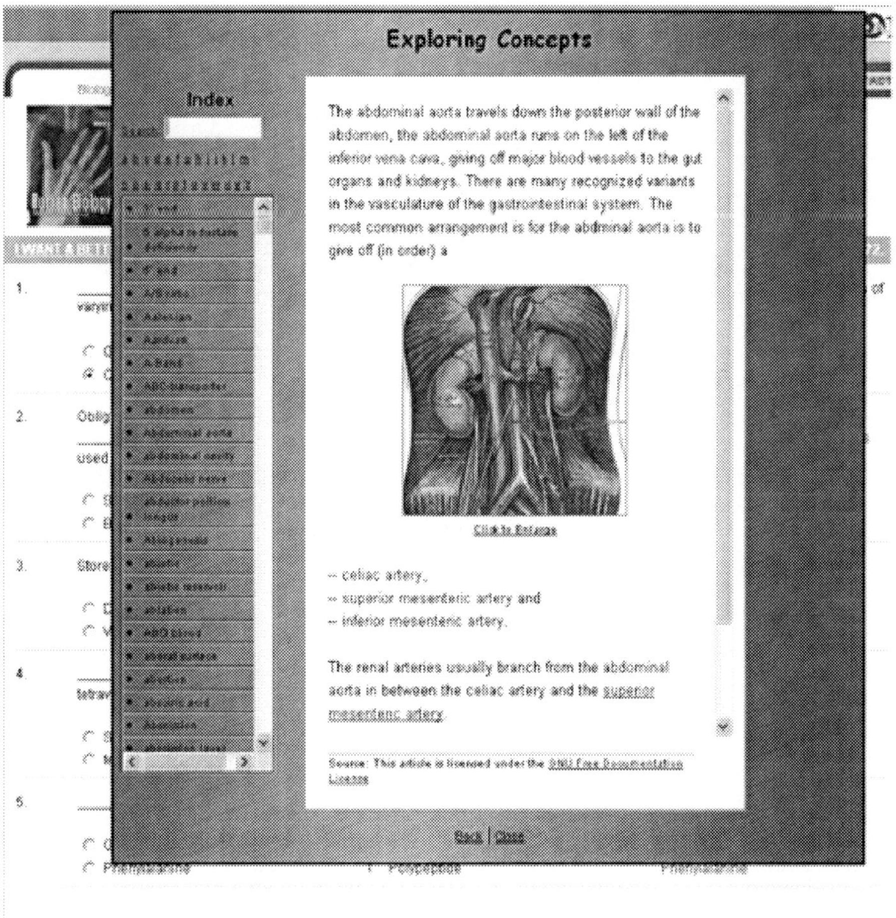

Visit **www.Cram101.com**, click Sign Up at the top of the screen, and enter DK73DW3607 in the promo code box on the registration screen. Access to www.Cram101.com is normally $9.95, but because you have purchased this book, your access fee is only $4.95. Sign up and stop highlighting textbooks forever.

Learning System

Cram101 Textbook Outlines is a learning system. The notes in this book are the highlights of your textbook, you will never have to highlight a book again.

How to use this book. Take this book to class, it is your notebook for the lecture. The notes and highlights on the left hand side of the pages follow the outline and order of the textbook. All you have to do is follow along while your intructor presents the lecture. Circle the items emphasized in class and add other important information on the right side. With Cram101 Textbook Outlines you'll spend less time writing and more time listening. Learning becomes more efficient.

Cram101.com Online

Increase your studying efficiency by using Cram101.com's practice tests and online reference material. It is the perfect complement to Cram101 Textbook Outlines. Use self-teaching matching tests or simulate in-class testing with comprehensive multiple choice tests, or simply use Cram's true and false tests for quick review. Cram101.com even allows you to enter your in-class notes for an integrated studying format combining the textbook notes with your class notes.

Visit **www.Cram101.com**, click Sign Up at the top of the screen, and enter **DK73DW3607** in the promo code box on the registration screen. Access to www.Cram101.com is normally $9.95, but because you have purchased this book, your access fee is only $4.95. Sign up and stop highlighting textbooks forever.

 ISBN: 1-4288-1820-0

Later Life: The Realities of Aging
Cox, 6th

CONTENTS

Social isolation	A type of loneliness that occurs when a person lacks a sense of integrated involvement. Being deprived of participation in a group or community involving companionship, shared interests, organized activities, and meaningful roles causes a person to feel is a social isolation.
Consciousness	The awareness of the senzations, thoughts, and feelings being experienced at a given moment is referred to as consciousness.
Government	A government is a body that has the authority to make and the power to enforce laws within a civil, corporate, religious, academic, or other organization or group.
Community	Community refers to a group of people who share a common sense of identity and interact with one another on a sustained basis.
Society	A society is a grouping of individuals, which is characterized by common interest and may have distinctive culture and institutions.
Disability	A physical or health condition that stigmatizes or causes discrimination, is referred to as a disability.
Social work	Social work is a helping profession focused on social change, problem solving in human relationships and the empowerment and liberation of people to enhance well-being.
Gerontology	Gerontology is the study of the elderly, and of the aging process itself.
Euthanasia	The act of painlessly ending the lives of persons who are suffering from incurable diseases or severe disabilities, sometimes called mercy killing, is referred to as euthanasia.
Hospice	A health care facility designed to counsel and care for the terminally ill is a hospice.
Crude birth rate	The number of live births per 1000 people in a population in a given year is a crude birth rate.
Baby Boomer	A baby boomer is someone who was born during the period of increased birth rates when economic prosperity rose in many countries following World War II. In the United States, the baby boomer term is commonly applied to people with birth years from the span 1946 to 1964, which may comprise more than one generation.
Census	A census is the process of obtaining information about every member of a population. It can be contrasted with sampling in which information is only obtained from a subset of a population. As such it is a method used for accumulating statistical data, and it is also vital to democracy.
Life expectancy	The number of years a newborn in a particular society can expect to live is referred to as a life expectancy.
Technology	The application of logic, reason and knowledge to the problems of exploiting raw materials from the environment, is referred to as a technology.
Mortality rate	Mortality rate is a measure of the number of deaths in some population, scaled to the size of that population, per unit time. Mortality rate is typically expressed in units of deaths per 1000 individuals per year; thus, a mortality rate of 10000.5 in a population of 100,000 would mean 1,000,500 deaths per year in the entire population.
Obesity	The state of being more than 20 percent above the average weight for a person of one's height is referred to as an obesity.
Statistics	Statistics is a mathematical science pertaining to the collection, analysis, interpretation, and presentation of data. It is applicable to a wide variety of academic disciplines, from the physical and social sciences to the humanities; it is also used and misused for making informed decisions in all areas of business and government.
Dementia	A global term for any neurological disorder in which the primary symptoms involve a deterioration of mental functioning is defined as dementia.

Depression	In the field of psychiatry, the word depression can also have this meaning of low mood but more specifically refers to a mental illness when it has reached a severity and duration to warrant a diagnosis, whether there is an obvious situational cause or not.
Dependency ratio	Dependency ratio refers to the ratio of people of dependent ages to people of economically active ages.
Labor force	Normally, the labor force consists of everyone of working age (typically above a certain age (around 14 to 16) and below retirement (around 65) who are participating workers, that is people actively employed or seeking employment.
Unemployment rate	In economics, one who is willing to work at a prevailing wage rate yet is unable to find a paying job is considered to be unemployed. The unemployment rate is the number of unemployed workers divided by the total civilian labor force, which includes both the unemployed and those with jobs (all those willing and able to work for pay).
Sex ratio	Sex ratio is the ratio of males to females in a population. The primary sex ratio is the ratio at the time of conception, secondary sex ratio is the ratio at time of birth. In humans the secondary sex ratio is commonly assumed to be 105 boys to 100 girls. In human societies, however, sex ratios at birth or among infants may be considerably skewed by sex-selective abortion and infanticide.
Marital status	A person's marital status describes their relationship with a significant other. Some common statuses are: married, single, separated, divorced, widowed, engaged, invalid, annulled, living common-law. The number of children may also be specified and, in this case, becomes synonymous with family status. For example: married with no children. Marital status is often a question on censuses, credit card applications, and many different polls.
Immigration	Although human migration has existed for hundreds of thousands of years, immigration in the modern sense refers to movement of people from one nation-state to another, where they are not citizens.
Significant other	Significant other is a gender-blind, politically correct term to refer to a person's partner in an intimate relationship without disclosing or presuming anything about his or her marital status or sexual orientation.
Prestige	Prestige refers to social respect accorded to an individual or group because of the status of their position.
Public health	Public health is concerned with threats to the overall health of a community based on population health analysis.
Oldest old	Oldest old refers to persons 85 years and older.
Late adulthood	The developmental period that lasts from about 60 to 70 years of age until death, is referred to as late adulthood.
Social structure	The term social structure, used in a general sense, refers to entities or groups in definite relation to each other, to relatively enduring patterns of behavior and relationship within social systems, or to social institutions and norms becoming embedded into social systems in such a way that they shape the behavior of actors within those social systems.
Mass society	Mass society is a society in which the concerns of the majority – the lower and middle social classes – play a prominent role, characterized by extension of voting rights, an improved standard of living for the lower classes and mass education.
Migration	The movement of people from one country or region to another in order to settle permanently, is referred to as a migration.
Longitudinal study	A type of developmental study in which the same group of participants is followed and measured at different ages is a longitudinal study.
Attitude	Attitude refers to an enduring mental representation of a person, place, or thing that evokes an emotional response and related behavior.

Go to **Cram101.com** for the Practice Tests for this Chapter.

Stereotype | A stereotype refers to widely shared beliefs about the characteristic traits, attitudes, and behaviors of members of various social groups, including the assumption that the members of such groups are usually all alike.

Social problem | A social condition that is perceived as having harmful effects is a social problem. Opinions about whether a condition is a social problem vary among groups and depend upon how and by whom the condition is defined and perceived in society.

Hierarchy | A hierarchy is a system of ranking and organizing things or people, where each element of the system (except for the top element) is subordinate to a single other element. A hierarchy can link entities either directly or indirectly, and either vertically or horizontally. The only direct links in a hierarchy are to one's immediate superior, or to one of one's subordinates.

Gerontology | Gerontology is the study of the elderly, and of the aging process itself.

Variable | A characteristic that varies in value or magnitude along which an object, individual or group may be categorized, such as income or age, is referred to as a variable.

Obesity | The state of being more than 20 percent above the average weight for a person of one's height is referred to as an obesity.

Random sample | A sample is a subset chosen from a population for investigation. A random sample is one chosen by a method involving an unpredictable component.

Disability | A physical or health condition that stigmatizes or causes discrimination, is referred to as a disability.

Social isolation | A type of loneliness that occurs when a person lacks a sense of integrated involvement. Being deprived of participation in a group or community involving companionship, shared interests, organized activities, and meaningful roles causes a person to feel is a social isolation.

Census | A census is the process of obtaining information about every member of a population. It can be contrasted with sampling in which information is only obtained from a subset of a population. As such it is a method used for accumulating statistical data, and it is also vital to democracy.

Government | A government is a body that has the authority to make and the power to enforce laws within a civil, corporate, religious, academic, or other organization or group.

Depression | In the field of psychiatry, the word depression can also have this meaning of low mood but more specifically refers to a mental illness when it has reached a severity and duration to warrant a diagnosis, whether there is an obvious situational cause or not.

Statistics | Statistics is a mathematical science pertaining to the collection, analysis, interpretation, and presentation of data. It is applicable to a wide variety of academic disciplines, from the physical and social sciences to the humanities; it is also used and misused for making informed decisions in all areas of business and government.

Social contact | Social contact is a pair of social actions with no further consequence - i.e. it is not likely to be repeated. It can sometimes be described as an accidental social interaction.

Industrial revolution | Industrial Revolution refers to the massive social, economic, and technological change in 18th and 19th century Great Britian. It commenced with the advent of the steam engine. Spread throughout Western Europe and North America in the 19th century.

Means of production | Means of production are the materials, tools and other instruments used by workers to make products. This includes: machines, tools materials, plant and equipment, land, raw materials, money, power generation, and so on: anything necessary for labor to produce.

Society | A society is a grouping of individuals, which is characterized by common interest and may

	have distinctive culture and institutions.
Mean	In statistics, mean has two related meanings: a)the average in ordinary English, which is also called the arithmetic mean (and is distinguished from the geometric mean or harmonic mean). The average is also called sample mean. b)the expected value of a random variable, which is also called the population mean.
Agricultural society	A society whose subsistence is based on the cultivation of plants using farming tools(ie. plow) is an agricultural society.
Stereotyping	Stereotyping refers to a process whereby a trait, usually negative, is generalized to all members of a particular group.
Motive	Motive refers to a hypothetical state within an organism that propels the organism toward a goal. In criminal law a motive is the cause that moves people and induce a certain action.
Ageism	Ageism refers to prejudice against a person on the grounds of age in the belief that the age category is inferior to other age categories and that unequal treatment is therefore justified.
Sexism	Sexism is commonly considered to be discrimination and/or hatred against people based on their sex rather than their individual merits, but can also refer to any and all systemic differentiations based on the sex of the individuals.
Racism	Racism is a belief in the moral or biological superiority of one race or ethnic group over another or others.
Community	Community refers to a group of people who share a common sense of identity and interact with one another on a sustained basis.
Social class	A category of people who occupy a similar position in relation to the means through which goods and services are produced in a society is a social class.
Neighborhood	A neighborhood is a geographically localized community located within a larger city, town or suburb. Traditionally, a neighborhood is small enough that the neighbors are all able to know each other.
Social interaction	Social interaction is a dynamic, changing sequence of social actions between individuals (or groups) who modify their actions and reactions due to the actions by their interaction partner(s). In other words they are events in which people attach meaning to a situation, interpret what others are meaning, and respond accordingly.
Labor force	Normally, the labor force consists of everyone of working age (typically above a certain age (around 14 to 16) and below retirement (around 65) who are participating workers, that is people actively employed or seeking employment.
Longitudinal study	A type of developmental study in which the same group of participants is followed and measured at different ages is a longitudinal study.
Mortality rate	Mortality rate is a measure of the number of deaths in some population, scaled to the size of that population, per unit time. Mortality rate is typically expressed in units of deaths per 1000 individuals per year; thus, a mortality rate of 10000.5 in a population of 100,000 would mean 1,000,500 deaths per year in the entire population.
Ghetto	A ghetto is an area where people from a specific racial or ethnic background or united in a given culture or religion live as a group, voluntarily or involuntarily, in milder or stricter seclusion.
Attitude	Attitude refers to an enduring mental representation of a person, place, or thing that evokes an emotional response and related behavior.

Go to **Cram101.com** for the Practice Tests for this Chapter.

Mass media | Mass media refers to forms of communication designed to reach a vast audience without any personal contact between the senders and receivers.

Murder | Murder is the unlawful, premeditated killing of a human being by another. The penalty for murder is usually either life imprisonment, or in jurisdictions with capital punishment, the death penalty.

Content analysis | Content analysis refers to analysis of words and images contained in written, spoken, and visual media.

Fear of crime | The fear of crime refers to the fear of being a victim of crime. Usually the fear is disproportionate to the likihood of being a victim of crime. Moral panics are often the cause of the rizing fear of crime.

Crime | Crime refers to any action that violates criminal laws established by political authority. A crime in a nontechnical sense is an act that violates a very important political or moral command.

Working class | Working class refers to a social class of industrial societies broadly composed of people involved in manual occupation.

Industrial society | In sociology, industrial society refers to a society with a modern societal structure. Such a structure developed in the west in the period of time following the industrial revolution. They are generally mass societies,

Discourse | In the social sciences, a discourse is considered to be an institutionalized way of thinking, a social boundary defining what can be said about a specific topic.

Mass society | Mass society is a society in which the concerns of the majority – the lower and middle social classes – play a prominent role, characterized by extension of voting rights, an improved standard of living for the lower classes and mass education.

Late adulthood | The developmental period that lasts from about 60 to 70 years of age until death, is referred to as late adulthood.

Social policy | Social policy relates to guidelines for the changing, maintenance or creation of living conditions that are conducive to human welfare. Thus social policy is that part of public policy that has to do with social issues such as public access to social programs.

Variable	A characteristic that varies in value or magnitude along which an object, individual or group may be categorized, such as income or age, is referred to as a variable.
Longitudinal study	A type of developmental study in which the same group of participants is followed and measured at different ages is a longitudinal study.
Cohort	A cohort is a group of subjects, most often humans from a given population, defined by experiencing an event (typically birth) in a particular time span.
Public opinion	Public opinion is the aggregate of individual attitudes or beliefs held by the adult population.
Attitude	Attitude refers to an enduring mental representation of a person, place, or thing that evokes an emotional response and related behavior.
Classism	Classism is any form of prejudice or oppression against people who are in, or who are perceived as being like those who are in, a lower social class (especially in the form of lower or higher socioeconomic status) within a class society.
Cohort effect	Effects on people's lives that arise from the characteristics of the historical periods during which they experienced stages of life such as childhood or middle age is known as a cohort effect.
Bias	A bias is a prejudice in a general or specific sense, usually in the sense for having a preference to one particular point of view or ideological perspective.
Fertility rate	The average number of children a woman can expect to have over her life, based on current rates of child-bearing is a fertility rate.
Labor force	Normally, the labor force consists of everyone of working age (typically above a certain age (around 14 to 16) and below retirement (around 65) who are participating workers, that is people actively employed or seeking employment.
Depression	In the field of psychiatry, the word depression can also have this meaning of low mood but more specifically refers to a mental illness when it has reached a severity and duration to warrant a diagnosis, whether there is an obvious situational cause or not.
Social institution	Social institution is a group of social positions, connected by social relations, performing a social role. It can be also defined in a narrow sense as any institution in a society that works to socialize the groups or people in it.
Organization	In sociology organization is understood as planned, coordinated and purposeful action of human beings to construct or compile a common tangible or intangible product or service.
Life chances	Life chances are the opportunities each individual has to improve their quality of life. The concept was introduced by German sociologist Max Weber. It is a probabilistic concept, describing how likely it is, given certain factors, that an individual's life will turn out a certain way.
Disengagement theory	Disengagement theory refers to the proposition that older persons make a normal and healthy adjustment to aging when they detach themselves from their social roles and prepare for their eventual death.
Gerontology	Gerontology is the study of the elderly, and of the aging process itself.
Society	A society is a grouping of individuals, which is characterized by common interest and may have distinctive culture and institutions.
Functionalism	In the social sciences, specifically sociology and sociocultural anthropology, functionalism, also called functional analysis, is a sociological perspective that originally attempted to explain social institutions as collective means to fill individual biological needs. Later,

	it came to focus on the ways in which social institutions fill social needs, especially social stability.
Social group	A group that consists of two or more people who interact frequently and share a common identity and a feeling of interdependence, is referred to as a social group.
Norm	In sociology, a norm, or social norm, is a rule that is socially enforced. Social sanctioning is what distinguishes norms from other cultural products such as meaning and values.
Community	Community refers to a group of people who share a common sense of identity and interact with one another on a sustained basis.
Neighborhood	A neighborhood is a geographically localized community located within a larger city, town or suburb. Traditionally, a neighborhood is small enough that the neighbors are all able to know each other.
Adaptation	Adaptation refers to the ability of a sociocultural system to change with the demands of a changing physical or social environment.
Social pressure	The entire set of psychological forces that are exerted on an individual by other people or by the individual's beliefs about other people is referred to as a social pressure.
Coping	Efforts to control, reduce, or learn to tolerate the threats that lead to stress is referred to as coping.
Activity Theory	The proposition that people tend to shift gears in late middle age and find substitutes for previous statuses, roles, and activities is referred to as activity theory.
Discrimination	Discrimination refers to the denial of equal access to social resources to people on the basis of their group membership.
Mean	In statistics, mean has two related meanings: a)the average in ordinary English, which is also called the arithmetic mean (and is distinguished from the geometric mean or harmonic mean). The average is also called sample mean. b)the expected value of a random variable, which is also called the population mean.
Latency	Latency refers to a phase of psychosexual development characterized by repression of sexual impulses.
Solidarity	Solidarity in sociology refers to the feeling or condition of unity based on common goals, interests, and sympathies among a group's members. Solidarity refers to the ties in a society - social relations - that bind people to one another.
Incest taboo	The 'Incest Taboo' refers to the prohibition, both formal and unstated, against incest, the practice of sexual relations between close blood relatives, in many societies. There are various theories that seek to explain how and why an incest taboo originates. Some advocates maintain that some sort of incest taboo is universal, while others dispute its universality.
Incest	Incest is sexual activity between close family members. Incest is considered taboo, and forbidden (fully or slightly) in the majority of current cultures.
Taboo	A taboo is a strong social prohibition (or ban) relating to any area of human activity or social custom declared as sacred and forbidden; breaking of the taboo is usually considered objectionable or abhorrent by society.
Adolescence	Adolescence is the transitional stage of human development in which a juvenile matures into an adult. This transition involves biological (i.e. pubertal), social, and psychological changes, though the biological ones are the easiest to measure objectively.
Identity crisis	Psychological state, identified by Erikson, in which youth face inner turmoil and uncertainty about life roles is an identity crisis.

Developmental theories	Those that assert that personal characteristics guide human development and influence behavioral choices but that these choices may change over the life course are called developmental theories.
Socialization	Socialization refers to the lifelong processes through which humans develop an awareness of social norms and values, and achieve a distinct sense of self.
Social change	Social change refers to alteration in social structures or culture over time.
Social movement	A social movement refers to large informal groupings of individuals and/or organizations focused on specific political or social issues, in other words, on carrying out, resisting or undoing a social change.
Prestige	Prestige refers to social respect accorded to an individual or group because of the status of their position.
Case Study	Case study refers to a research design that focuses on a single example rather than a representative sample.
Age Stratification	Age stratification refers to the inequalities, differences, segregation, or conflict between age groups.
Caste	Caste refers to a closed form of stratification in which an individual's status is determined by birth and cannot be changed.
Industrial society	In sociology, industrial society refers to a society with a modern societal structure. Such a structure developed in the west in the period of time following the industrial revolution. They are generally mass societies,
Social position	The social identity an individual has in a given group or society, where social positions may be general in nature or may be more specific, is referred to as a social position.
Sex ratio	Sex ratio is the ratio of males to females in a population. The primary sex ratio is the ratio at the time of conception, secondary sex ratio is the ratio at time of birth. In humans the secondary sex ratio is commonly assumed to be 105 boys to 100 girls. In human societies, however, sex ratios at birth or among infants may be considerably skewed by sex-selective abortion and infanticide.
Status group	The sociologist Max Weber formulated a three-component theory of stratification in which he defines status group (also known as a status class) as a group of people (part of a society) that can be differentiated on the basis of non-economical qualities like honour, prestige and religion.
Empirical study	An empirical study in social sciences is when the research ends are based on evidence and not just theory. This is done to comply with the scientific method that asserts the objective discovery of knowledge based on verifiable facts of evidence.
Social class	A category of people who occupy a similar position in relation to the means through which goods and services are produced in a society is a social class.
Minority group	A minority group or subordinate group is a sociological group that does not constitute a politically dominant plurality of the total population of a given society.
Subculture	A group within the broader society that has values, norms and lifestyle distinct from those of the majority, is referred to as a subculture.
Social interaction	Social interaction is a dynamic, changing sequence of social actions between individuals (or groups) who modify their actions and reactions due to the actions by their interaction partner(s). In other words they are events in which people attach meaning to a situation, interpret what others are meaning, and respond accordingly.

Social relation	Social relation can refer to a multitude of social interactions, regulated by social norms, between two or more people, with each having a social position and performing a social role.
Social environment	The social environment is the direct influence of a group of individuals and their contributions to this environment, as both groups and individuals who are in frequent communication with each other within their cultural or socio-economical strata, which create role identity(-ies) and guide the individual's self (sociology) growth and their progression towards maturity.
Compliance	Conforming behavior that occurs in response to direct social pressure is referred to as compliance.
Reciprocity	In social psychology, reciprocity refers to in-kind positive or negative responses of individuals towards the actions of others. Thus positively interpreted actions elicit positive responses and vice versa.
Symbolic interaction	Symbolic interaction refers to the use of symbols by people to present themselves to others and interpret one another's behavior.
George Mead	George Mead is an important figure in 20th century social philosophy. His theory of how the mind and self emerge from the social process of communication by signs founded the symbolic interactionist school of sociology and social psychology.
Cooley	Cooley was an American sociologist whose concept of the "looking glass self" is undoubtedly his most famous, and is known and accepted by most psychologists and sociologists today. It expanded William James's idea of self to include the capacity of reflection on its own behavior. Other people's views build, change and maintain our self-image; thus, there is an interaction between how we see ourselves and how others see us.
Acquisition	The initial learning of the stimulus response link, which involves a neutral stimulus being associated with a UCS and becoming a conditioned stimulus, is referred to as an acquisition.
Symbolic interaction theory	Symbolic interaction theory refers to a theory that describes the family as a unit of interacting personalities communicating through symbols.
Social behavior	Social behavior is behavior directed towards, or taking place between, members of the same species.
Collective behavior	Collective behavior refers to the relatively unstructured behavior of people in crowds and masses, which is often a voluntary, spontaneous, activity that is engaged in by a large number of people and typically violates dominant group norms and values.
Social psychology	Social psychology refers to the study of the effects of social environments on the psychological functioning of individuals.
Social development	Social development is a type of a social process which leads to structural transformations of social systems.
Labeling theory	A social theory that holds that society's reaction to certain behaviors is a major factor in defining the self as deviant is labeling theory.
Labeling	Labeling is defining or describing a person in terms of his or her behavior. The term is often used in sociology to describe human interaction, control and identification of deviant behavior.
Significant other	Significant other is a gender-blind, politically correct term to refer to a person's partner in an intimate relationship without disclosing or presuming anything about his or her marital status or sexual orientation.
Disengagement	A theory that holds that aging is a gradual withdrawal from the world on physical,

theory of aging	psychological, and social level, is referred to as a disengagement theory of aging.
Social forces	Social forces are the typical basic drives, or motives, which lead to the fundamental types of association and group relationship.
Social structure	The term social structure, used in a general sense, refers to entities or groups in definite relation to each other, to relatively enduring patterns of behavior and relationship within social systems, or to social institutions and norms becoming embedded into social systems in such a way that they shape the behavior of actors within those social systems.
Metropolitan area	A metropolitan area is a large population center consisting of a large city and its adjacent zone of influence, or of several neighboring cities or towns and adjoining areas, with one or more large cities serving as its hub or hubs.
Sociometry	The study of patterns of affection and loyalty that bind some group members more closely than others, is referred to as sociometry.
Sociocultural perspective	The view that focuses on the roles of ethnicity, gender, culture, and socioeconomic status in personality formation, behavior, and mental processes is a sociocultural perspective.
Social stratification	The systematic, uneven distribution of valued products of social life such as wealth, power, and prestige among the occupants of different social statuses, is referred to as a social stratification.
Activity Theory of Aging	Activity theory of aging refers to a theory that holds that the elderly who age most successfully are those who maintain the interests and activities they had during middle age.
Role theory	Role theory refers to a theory that explains hypnotic events in terms of the person's ability to act as though he or she were hypnotized. Role theory differs from faking in that subjects cooperate and focus on hypnotic suggestions instead of pretending to be hypnotized.
Voluntary association	A voluntary association is a group of individuals who voluntarily enter into an agreement to form a body (or organization) to accomplish a purpose.

Society — A society is a grouping of individuals, which is characterized by common interest and may have distinctive culture and institutions.

Variable — A characteristic that varies in value or magnitude along which an object, individual or group may be categorized, such as income or age, is referred to as a variable.

Cohort — A cohort is a group of subjects, most often humans from a given population, defined by experiencing an event (typically birth) in a particular time span.

Life expectancy — The number of years a newborn in a particular society can expect to live is referred to as a life expectancy.

Census — A census is the process of obtaining information about every member of a population. It can be contrasted with sampling in which information is only obtained from a subset of a population. As such it is a method used for accumulating statistical data, and it is also vital to democracy.

Classism — Classism is any form of prejudice or oppression against people who are in, or who are perceived as being like those who are in, a lower social class (especially in the form of lower or higher socioeconomic status) within a class society.

Social evolution — Social evolution refers to theories of social change which generally hold that human societies move from simple to complex forms of organization.

Elite — The elite is a relatively small dominant group within a larger society, which enjoys a privileged status which is upheld by individuals of lower social status within the structure of a group.

Government — A government is a body that has the authority to make and the power to enforce laws within a civil, corporate, religious, academic, or other organization or group.

Demographic transition — A stabilization of population level in industrial society once a certain level of economic prosperity has been reached, is referred to as a demographic transition.

Population growth — Population growth is change in population over time, and can be quantified as the change in the number of individuals in a population per unit time. The term population growth can technically refer to any species, but almost always refers to humans, and it is often used informally for the more specific demographic term population growth rate , and is often used to refer specifically to the growth of the population of the world.

Agricultural society — A society whose subsistence is based on the cultivation of plants using farming tools(ie. plow) is an agricultural society.

Attitude — Attitude refers to an enduring mental representation of a person, place, or thing that evokes an emotional response and related behavior.

Mean — In statistics, mean has two related meanings: a)the average in ordinary English, which is also called the arithmetic mean (and is distinguished from the geometric mean or harmonic mean). The average is also called sample mean. b)the expected value of a random variable, which is also called the population mean.

Norm — In sociology, a norm, or social norm, is a rule that is socially enforced. Social sanctioning is what distinguishes norms from other cultural products such as meaning and values.

Developed country — A developed country is a term used to categorise countries with developed economies, ones in which the tertiary and quaternary sectors of industry dominate. This level of economic development usually translates into a high income per capita, and a high Human Development Index (HDI). Countries with high gross domestic product (GDP) per capita often fit the previous description of a developed economy; however, anomalies exist when determining "developed" status by the factor GDP/cap alone.

Modernization	The process of general social change brought about by the transition from an agrarian to an industrial mode of production, is referred to as modernization.
Gerontology	Gerontology is the study of the elderly, and of the aging process itself.
Third world	Third world refers to societies in which industrial production is only developed to a limited degree.
Industrial society	In sociology, industrial society refers to a society with a modern societal structure. Such a structure developed in the west in the period of time following the industrial revolution. They are generally mass societies,
Kinship	Kinship is the most basic principle of organizing individuals into social groups, roles, and categories. It was originally thought to be determined by biological descent, a view that was challenged by David M. Schneider in his work on Symbolic Kinship.
Organization	In sociology organization is understood as planned, coordinated and purposeful action of human beings to construct or compile a common tangible or intangible product or service.
Property rights	Socially recognized rights of an individual over economic assets, including physical objects, land, currency and credit, and labor are property rights.
Means of production	Means of production are the materials, tools and other instruments used by workers to make products. This includes: machines, tools materials, plant and equipment, land, raw materials, money, power generation, and so on: anything necessary for labor to produce.
Acquisition	The initial learning of the stimulus response link, which involves a neutral stimulus being associated with a UCS and becoming a conditioned stimulus, is referred to as an acquisition.
Modernization theory	Modernization theory is a socio-economic theory, sometimes known as (or as being encompassed within) development theory, which highlights the positive role played by the developed world in modernizing and facilitating sustainable development in underdeveloped nations.
Community	Community refers to a group of people who share a common sense of identity and interact with one another on a sustained basis.
Industrializ-tion	Industrialization is a process of social and economic change whereby a human society is transformed from a pre-industrial (an economy where the amount of capital accumulated is low) to an industrial state
Authority	Authority refers to power that is attached to a position that others perceive as legitimate.
Extended family	Extended family refers to a family group consisting of more than two generations of the same kinship line living either within the same household or, more usually in the west, very close to one another.
Family disruption	Family disruption refers to the behaviors associated with altering or terminating family and pseudo-family units; separation, annulment, divorce, disownment, death, etc.
Romantic love	Romantic love is a form of love that is often regarded as different from mere needs driven by sexual desire, or lust. Romantic love generally involves a mix of emotional and sexual desire, as opposed to Platonic love. There is often, initially, more emphasis on the emotions than on physical pleasure.
Labor force	Normally, the labor force consists of everyone of working age (typically above a certain age (around 14 to 16) and below retirement (around 65) who are participating workers, that is people actively employed or seeking employment.
Nuclear family	The term nuclear family was developed in the western world to distinguish the family group consisting of parents and their children, usually a father, mother, and children, from what is known as an extended family.

Socialization Socialization refers to the lifelong processes through which humans develop an awareness of social norms and values, and achieve a distinct sense of self.

Ritual A ritual is a set of actions, performed mainly for their symbolic value, which is prescribed by a religion or by the traditions of a community.

Technology The application of logic, reason and knowledge to the problems of exploiting raw materials from the environment, is referred to as a technology.

Social change Social change refers to alteration in social structures or culture over time.

Consequent Consequent refers to the second of two propositions in a logical argument of the form If antecedent is true, then consequent follows.

Systems theory A theory that emphasizes the interdependence of family members and how they affect one another is a systems theory.

Goffman Goffman was one of the most influential sociologists of the twentieth century, on a par with Weber, Durkheim, Marx, and Mead, in whose footsteps he followed in developing a sociological social psychology. His greatest contribution to social theory is his formulation of symbolic interaction in his 1959 book The Presentation of Self in Everyday Life.

Industrialized societies Strongly developed nation-states in which the majority of the population work in factories or offices rather than in agriculture, and most people live in urban areas are referred to as industrialized societies.

Political system A political system or political institution is a social system of politics and government. It is usually compared to the law system, economic system, cultural system, and other social systems.

Interdependence Interdependence is a dynamic of being mutually responsible to and sharing a common set of principles with others. This concept differs dinstinctly from "dependence" in that an interdependent relationship implies that all participants are emotionally, economically, and/or morally "independent."

Agrarian society An agrarian society is one that is based on agriculture as its prime means for support and sustenance. The society acknowledges other means of livelihood and work habits but stresses on agriculture and farming, and was the main form of socio-economic organization for most of recorded human history.

Social role A social role is a set of connected behaviors, rights and obligations as conceptualized by actors in a social situation. It is mostly defined as an expected behavior in a given individual social status and social position.

Conjugal family A conjugal family is nuclear family of adult partners and their children (by birth or adoption) where the family relationship is principally focused inwardly and ties to extended kin are voluntary and based on emotional bonds, rather than strict duties and obligations.This considers the spouses and their children as of prime importance and which has a fringe of comparatively unimportant relatives. The marriage bond is important and stressed.

Abkhasia Abkhazia is a region of 8,600 km² (3,300 sq mi.) in the Caucasus, which is de jure an autonomous republic of Georgia, but which proclaimed independence after a war in the early 1990s. Although it is not recognized internationally as a separate nation, Abkhazia remains largely de facto independent of Georgia and maintains control over a large part of its territory, including the capital of Sukhumi on the Black Sea

Obesity The state of being more than 20 percent above the average weight for a person of one's height is referred to as an obesity.

Prestige — Prestige refers to social respect accorded to an individual or group because of the status of their position.

Achieved Status — Achieved status is a sociological term denoting a social position that a person assumes voluntarily which reflects personal skills, abilities, and efforts.

Intake — Intake refers to process during which a juvenile referral is received and a decision is made to file a petition in juvenile court to release the juvenile, to place the juvenile under supervision, or to refer the juvenile elsewhere.

Ascribed status — Ascribed status is a social status a person is given from birth or assumes involuntarily later in life. For example, a person born into a wealthy family has a high ascribed status.

Punishment — Punishment is the practice of imposing something unpleasant on a subject as a response to some unwanted behavior or disobedience that the subject has displayed.

Division of labor — Division of labor is the specialisation of cooperative labor in specific, circumscribed tasks and roles, intended to increase efficiency of output.

Gerontocracy — A gerontocracy is a form of oligarchical rule in which an entity is ruled by leaders who are significantly older than most of the adult population. Often the political structure is such that political power within the ruling class accumulates with age, so that the oldest hold the most power.

Symbolic interaction — Symbolic interaction refers to the use of symbols by people to present themselves to others and interpret one another's behavior.

Ancestor Worship — The religious worship of ancestors based on the belief that they possess supernatural power is referred to as an ancestor worship.

Anthropology — A social science, closely linked to sociology, which concentrates on the study of traditional cultures--particularly hunting and gathering, horticultural societies, and the evolution of the human species is referred to as anthropology.

Family study — A scientific study in which researchers assess hereditary influence by examining blood relatives to see how much they resemble each other on a specific trait is a family study.

Putnam — Putnam makes a distinction between two kinds of social capital: bonding capital and bridging capital. Bonding occurs when you are socializing with people who are like you: same age, same race, same religion, and so on. But in order to create peaceful societies in a diverse multi-ethnic country, one needs to have a second kind of social capital: bridging.

Presentation of self — Goffman's term for people's efforts to present themselves to others in ways that are most favorable to their own interests or image, is referred to as a presentation of self.

Mass society — Mass society is a society in which the concerns of the majority – the lower and middle social classes – play a prominent role, characterized by extension of voting rights, an improved standard of living for the lower classes and mass education.

Malthus — Malthus is best known for his pessimistic, often false, but highly influential views on population growth. It is this theory of Malthus—not some easily dismissed prediction—that has had huge influence on evolutionary theory in both biology (as acknowledged by Darwin and Wallace) and the social sciences (such as Spencer). Malthus's population theory has also profoundly affected the modern day ecological-evolutionary social theory of Gerhard Lenski and Marvin Harris. He can thus be regarded as an element of the canon of socioeconomic theory.

Social structure — The term social structure, used in a general sense, refers to entities or groups in definite relation to each other, to relatively enduring patterns of behavior and relationship within social systems, or to social institutions and norms becoming embedded into social systems in

such a way that they shape the behavior of actors within those social systems.

Variable | A characteristic that varies in value or magnitude along which an object, individual or group may be categorized, such as income or age, is referred to as a variable.

Intake | Intake refers to process during which a juvenile referral is received and a decision is made to file a petition in juvenile court to release the juvenile, to place the juvenile under supervision, or to refer the juvenile elsewhere.

Social skill | A social skill is a skill used to interact and communicate with others to assist status in the social structure and other motivations. Social rules and social relations are created, communicated, and changed in verbal and nonverbal ways creating social complexity useful in identifying outsiders and intelligent breeding partners.

Disability | A physical or health condition that stigmatizes or causes discrimination, is referred to as a disability.

Mortality rate | Mortality rate is a measure of the number of deaths in some population, scaled to the size of that population, per unit time. Mortality rate is typically expressed in units of deaths per 1000 individuals per year; thus, a mortality rate of 10000.5 in a population of 100,000 would mean 1,000,500 deaths per year in the entire population.

Life chances | Life chances are the opportunities each individual has to improve their quality of life. The concept was introduced by German sociologist Max Weber. It is a probabilistic concept, describing how likely it is, given certain factors, that an individual's life will turn out a certain way.

Life expectancy | The number of years a newborn in a particular society can expect to live is referred to as a life expectancy.

Immunity | Immunity confers a status on a person or body that places him/her/it above the law and makes that person or body free from otherwise legal obligations such as, for example, liability for torts or damages or prosecution under criminal law for criminal acts.

Statistics | Statistics is a mathematical science pertaining to the collection, analysis, interpretation, and presentation of data. It is applicable to a wide variety of academic disciplines, from the physical and social sciences to the humanities; it is also used and misused for making informed decisions in all areas of business and government.

Tolerance | Tolerance is a recent political term used within debates in areas of social, cultural and religious context, as an emphatic antithesis to discrimination, as such may advocate persecution. Its usage came about as a more widely acceptable alternative to "acceptance", the usage of which had been widely derided, as certain cases would not be considered by common society as acceptable.

Battery | In many common law jurisdictions, the crime of battery involves an injury or other contact upon the person of another in a manner likely to cause bodily harm.

Social pressure | The entire set of psychological forces that are exerted on an individual by other people or by the individual's beliefs about other people is referred to as a social pressure.

Social role | A social role is a set of connected behaviors, rights and obligations as conceptualized by actors in a social situation. It is mostly defined as an expected behavior in a given individual social status and social position.

Evolutionary perspective | A perspective that focuses on how humans have evolved and adapted behaviors required for survival against various environmental pressures over the long course of evolution is an evolutionary perspective.

Mean | In statistics, mean has two related meanings: a)the average in ordinary English, which is also called the arithmetic mean (and is distinguished from the geometric mean or harmonic mean). The average is also called sample mean. b)the expected value of a random variable,

	which is also called the population mean.
Antigen	An antigen is a substance that stimulates an immune response, especially the production of antibodies. They are usually proteins or polysaccharides, but can be any type of molecule, including small molecules (haptens) coupled to a carrier-protein.
Dependent variable	A variable affected by another variable, is referred to as a dependent variable.
Social isolation	A type of loneliness that occurs when a person lacks a sense of integrated involvement. Being deprived of participation in a group or community involving companionship, shared interests, organized activities, and meaningful roles causes a person to feel is a social isolation.
Mental hospital	A medical institution specializing in providing inpatient care for psychological disorders is a psychiatric hospital or mental hospital.
Reference group	Individuals almost universally have a bond toward a Reference Group. These are groups to which the individual does not have real membership, but to which he conceptually relates him/herself, and from which he might accept goals and values as a part of his/her self identity.
Significant other	Significant other is a gender-blind, politically correct term to refer to a person's partner in an intimate relationship without disclosing or presuming anything about his or her marital status or sexual orientation.
Reconstruction	Reconstruction refers to a memory that is not an exact replica of an event but has been pieced together from a few highlights, using information that may or may not be accurate.
Placebo effect	A placebo effect occurs when a patient's symptoms are altered in some way (i.e., alleviated or exacerbated) by an otherwise inert treatment, due to the individual expecting or believing that it will work. Some people consider this to be a remarkable aspect of human physiology; others consider it to be an illusion arizing from the way experiments are conducted.
Labeling	Labeling is defining or describing a person in terms of his or her behavior. The term is often used in sociology to describe human interaction, control and identification of deviant behavior.
Coping	Efforts to control, reduce, or learn to tolerate the threats that lead to stress is referred to as coping.
Society	A society is a grouping of individuals, which is characterized by common interest and may have distinctive culture and institutions.
Sick role	Sick role was a concept invented by Talcott Parsons that refers to patterns of behavior expected of one who is sick and this role often exempts the person from their normal role obligations.
Parsons	Parsons was an advocate of "grand theory," an attempt to integrate all the social sciences into an overarching theoretical framework. His early work — The Structure of Social Action —reviewed the output of his great predecessors, especially Max Weber, Vilfredo Pareto, and Émile Durkheim, and attempted to derive from them a single "action theory" based on the assumptions that human action is voluntary, intentional, and symbolic.
Community	Community refers to a group of people who share a common sense of identity and interact with one another on a sustained basis.
Attitude	Attitude refers to an enduring mental representation of a person, place, or thing that evokes an emotional response and related behavior.
Social movement	A social movement refers to large informal groupings of individuals and/or organizations focused on specific political or social issues, in other words, on carrying out, resisting or

	undoing a social change.
Biomedical Model	A perspective that focuses on illness rather than on health, explaining illness in terms of biological factors without regard to psychological and social factors is defined as a biomedical model.
Group therapy	Group therapy is a form of psychotherapy during which one or several therapists treat a small group of clients together as a group. This may be more cost effective than individual therapy, and possibly even more productive.
Obesity	The state of being more than 20 percent above the average weight for a person of one's height is referred to as an obesity.
Depression	In the field of psychiatry, the word depression can also have this meaning of low mood but more specifically refers to a mental illness when it has reached a severity and duration to warrant a diagnosis, whether there is an obvious situational cause or not.
Cohort	A cohort is a group of subjects, most often humans from a given population, defined by experiencing an event (typically birth) in a particular time span.
Social behavior	Social behavior is behavior directed towards, or taking place between, members of the same species.
Social psychology	Social psychology refers to the study of the effects of social environments on the psychological functioning of individuals.
Preventive medicine	Generally speaking, preventive medicine is that part of medicine engaged with preventing disease rather than curing it. It can be contrasted not only with curative medicine, but also with public health methods which work at the level of population health rather than individual health.
Technology	The application of logic, reason and knowledge to the problems of exploiting raw materials from the environment, is referred to as a technology.
Public health	Public health is concerned with threats to the overall health of a community based on population health analysis.
Mode	In statistics, mode means the most frequent value assumed by a random variable, or occurring in a sampling of a random variable.
Gerontology	Gerontology is the study of the elderly, and of the aging process itself.

Symbolic interaction
Symbolic interaction refers to the use of symbols by people to present themselves to others and interpret one another's behavior.

Frame of reference
One's unique patterning of perceptions and attitudes according to which one evaluates and reacts to events is a frame of reference.

Life history
Life history refers to a variety of methods and techniques that are used for conducting qualitative interviews. The method was first used when interviewing indigenous peoples of the Americas.

Social change
Social change refers to alteration in social structures or culture over time.

Adaptation
Adaptation refers to the ability of a sociocultural system to change with the demands of a changing physical or social environment.

Longitudinal study
A type of developmental study in which the same group of participants is followed and measured at different ages is a longitudinal study.

Psychosis
A serious mental disorder that involves a failure to distinguish between internal and external reality, in which the affected person cannot function effectively in social life is referred to as psychosis.

Control group
A group of people in an experiment who are not exposed to the experimental stimulus under study are referred to as a control group.

Oldest old
Oldest old refers to persons 85 years and older.

Prejudice
Prejudice is, as the name implies, the process of "pre-judging" something. It implies coming to a judgment on a subject before learning where the preponderance of evidence actually lies, or forming a judgment without direct experience.

Dementia
A global term for any neurological disorder in which the primary symptoms involve a deterioration of mental functioning is defined as dementia.

Variable
A characteristic that varies in value or magnitude along which an object, individual or group may be categorized, such as income or age, is referred to as a variable.

Life chances
Life chances are the opportunities each individual has to improve their quality of life. The concept was introduced by German sociologist Max Weber. It is a probabilistic concept, describing how likely it is, given certain factors, that an individual's life will turn out a certain way.

Norm
In sociology, a norm, or social norm, is a rule that is socially enforced. Social sanctioning is what distinguishes norms from other cultural products such as meaning and values.

Reciprocity
In social psychology, reciprocity refers to in-kind positive or negative responses of individuals towards the actions of others. Thus positively interpreted actions elicit positive responses and vice versa.

Socialization
Socialization refers to the lifelong processes through which humans develop an awareness of social norms and values, and achieve a distinct sense of self.

Social role
A social role is a set of connected behaviors, rights and obligations as conceptualized by actors in a social situation. It is mostly defined as an expected behavior in a given individual social status and social position.

Range
A measure of variability defined as the high score in a distribution minus the low score is referred to as a range.

Carson
In addition to individualist anarchist Benjamin Tucker's "big four" monopolies (land, money, tariffs, and patents), Carson argues that the state has also transferred wealth to the wealthy by subsidizing organizational centralization, in the form of transportation and

	communication subsidies. He believes that Tucker overlooked this issue due to Tucker's focus on individual market transactions, whereas Carson also focuses on organizational issues.
Social structure	The term social structure, used in a general sense, refers to entities or groups in definite relation to each other, to relatively enduring patterns of behavior and relationship within social systems, or to social institutions and norms becoming embedded into social systems in such a way that they shape the behavior of actors within those social systems.
Social behavior	Social behavior is behavior directed towards, or taking place between, members of the same species.
Coping	Efforts to control, reduce, or learn to tolerate the threats that lead to stress is referred to as coping.
Social pressure	The entire set of psychological forces that are exerted on an individual by other people or by the individual's beliefs about other people is referred to as a social pressure.
Typology	Typology refers to the classification of observations in terms of their attributes on two or more variables. The classification of newspapers as liberal-urban, liberal-rural, conservative-urban, or conservative-rural would be an example of a typology.
Disengagement theory	Disengagement theory refers to the proposition that older persons make a normal and healthy adjustment to aging when they detach themselves from their social roles and prepare for their eventual death.
Activity Theory	The proposition that people tend to shift gears in late middle age and find substitutes for previous statuses, roles, and activities is referred to as activity theory.
Reference group	Individuals almost universally have a bond toward a Reference Group. These are groups to which the individual does not have real membership, but to which he conceptually relates him/herself, and from which he might accept goals and values as a part of his/her self identity.
Cohort	A cohort is a group of subjects, most often humans from a given population, defined by experiencing an event (typically birth) in a particular time span.
Validity	The degree to which a measurement instrument measures what it is intended to measure is referred to as validity.
Alarm Reaction	The first stage of the general adaptation syndrome, which is triggered by the impact of a stressor and characterized by sympathetic activity, is referred to as an alarm reaction.
Depression	In the field of psychiatry, the word depression can also have this meaning of low mood but more specifically refers to a mental illness when it has reached a severity and duration to warrant a diagnosis, whether there is an obvious situational cause or not.
Social network	A social network is a social structure made of nodes which are generally individuals or organizations. It indicates the ways in which they are connected through various social familiarities ranging from casual acquaintance to close familial bonds.
Negative relationship	A relationship in which high scores on one variable are related to low scores on another is a negative relationship.
Socioeconomic status	An overall rank based on characteristics such as education and occupation, used to describe people's positions in stratification systems is referred to as socioeconomic status.
Community	Community refers to a group of people who share a common sense of identity and interact with one another on a sustained basis.
Disability	A physical or health condition that stigmatizes or causes discrimination, is referred to as a

	disability.
Poverty line	The poverty threshold, or poverty line, is the level of income below which one cannot afford to purchase all the resources one requires to live. Thus, by definition, nobody lives below the poverty line.
Personality disorder	Personality disorder refers to a mental disorder characterized by a set of inflexible, maladaptive personality traits that keep a person from functioning properly in society.
Alcoholism	Alcoholism refers to a disorder that involves long-term, repeated, uncontrolled, compulsive, and excessive use of alcoholic beverages and that impairs the drinker's health, work and social relationships.
Substance abuse	Substance abuse refers to the overindulgence in and dependence on a psychoactive leading to effects that are detrimental to the individual's physical health or mental health, or the welfare of others.
Early onset	Early onset refers to the outbreak of deviant or delinquent behavior in preadolescence, which is generally viewed as a precursor of chronic offending in adolescence and which generally continues into adulthood.
Psychotherapy	Psychotherapy refers to a systematic interaction between a therapist and a client that brings psychological principles to bear on influencing the client's thoughts, feelings, or behavior to help that client overcome abnormal behavior or adjust to problems in living.
Antidepressant	An antidepressant is a medication designed to treat or alleviate the symptoms of clinical depression. Some, notably the tricyclics, are commonly used off-label in the treatment of neuropathic pain, whether or not the patient is depressed. Smaller doses are generally used for this purpose, and they often take effect more quickly.
Insanity	Insanity refers to a legal status indicating that a person cannot be held responsible for his or her actions because of mental illness.
Acetylcholine	A neurotransmitter used by somatic neurons that contract the body's large muscles and by neurons in the brain that apparently regulate wakefulness and dream sleep is referred to as acetylcholine. It also plays a role in learning, memory, and rapid eye movement sleep and causes the skeletal muscle fibers to contract.
Society	A society is a grouping of individuals, which is characterized by common interest and may have distinctive culture and institutions.
Late adulthood	The developmental period that lasts from about 60 to 70 years of age until death, is referred to as late adulthood.
Epidemiology	Epidemiology is the scientific study of factors affecting the health and illness of populations, and serves as the foundation and logic of interventions made in the interest of public health and preventive medicine.
Social psychology	Social psychology refers to the study of the effects of social environments on the psychological functioning of individuals.
Gerontology	Gerontology is the study of the elderly, and of the aging process itself.
Social theory	Social theory refers to the use of theoretical frameworks to explain and analyze social patterns and large-scale social structures. Social theory attempts to answer the question 'what is?', not 'what should be?'. One should therefore not confuse it with philosophy or with belief.
Social readjustment rating scale	Social readjustment rating scale refers to Holmes and Rahe's stress scale, which ranks 43 life events from most to least stressful and assigns a point value to each.

Consensus — Agreement on basic social values by the members of a group or society is referred to as a consensus.

Attitude — Attitude refers to an enduring mental representation of a person, place, or thing that evokes an emotional response and related behavior.

Case Study — Case study refers to a research design that focuses on a single example rather than a representative sample.

Social change	Social change refers to alteration in social structures or culture over time.
Socialization	Socialization refers to the lifelong processes through which humans develop an awareness of social norms and values, and achieve a distinct sense of self.
Society	A society is a grouping of individuals, which is characterized by common interest and may have distinctive culture and institutions.
Anticipatory socialization	The process of learning how to perform a role attached to a status we do not yet occupy is referred to as anticipatory socialization.
Norm	In sociology, a norm, or social norm, is a rule that is socially enforced. Social sanctioning is what distinguishes norms from other cultural products such as meaning and values.
Social environment	The social environment is the direct influence of a group of individuals and their contributions to this environment, as both groups and individuals who are in frequent communication with each other within their cultural or socio-economical strata, which create role identity(-ies) and guide the individual's self (sociology) growth and their progression towards maturity.
Neighborhood	A neighborhood is a geographically localized community located within a larger city, town or suburb. Traditionally, a neighborhood is small enough that the neighbors are all able to know each other.
Social comparison	The process through which we compare ourselves to others in order to determine whether our view of social reality is or is not correct, is referred to as a social comparison.
Dominance	In animal colonies, a condition established by one animal over another by prevailing in an aggressive encounter between the two, is referred to as dominance.
Range	A measure of variability defined as the high score in a distribution minus the low score is referred to as a range.
Community	Community refers to a group of people who share a common sense of identity and interact with one another on a sustained basis.
Gender	Gender refers to socially defined behavior regarded as appropriate for the members of each
Role performance	The actual behavior of people who occupy a status is referred to as a role performance.
Social pressure	The entire set of psychological forces that are exerted on an individual by other people or by the individual's beliefs about other people is referred to as a social pressure.
Social constraint	Social constraint refers to the conditioning influence of the groups and societies of which we are a part on our behavior. Social constraint was regarded by Emile Durkheim as one of the distinctive properties of social facts.
Cohort	A cohort is a group of subjects, most often humans from a given population, defined by experiencing an event (typically birth) in a particular time span.
Attitude	Attitude refers to an enduring mental representation of a person, place, or thing that evokes an emotional response and related behavior.
Deviant behavior	Deviant behavior is behavior that is a recognized violation of social norms. Formal and informal social controls attempt to prevent and minimize deviance. One such control is through the medicalization of deviance.
Conformity	Conformity is the act of consciously maintaining a certain degree of similarity (in clothing, manners, behaviors, etc.) to those in your general social circles, to those in authority, or to the general status quo. Usually, conformity implies a tendency to submit to others in thought and behavior other than simply clothing choice.

Typology	Typology refers to the classification of observations in terms of their attributes on two or more variables. The classification of newspapers as liberal-urban, liberal-rural, conservative-urban, or conservative-rural would be an example of a typology.
Merton	Merton coined the phrase "self-fulfilling prophecy." He also coined many other phrases that have gone into everyday use, such as "role model" and "unintended consequences".
Ritualism	Outward conformity to norms without a commitment to values they support is ritualism.
Retreatism	A form of deviance in which a person withdraws from social life by rejecting values and norms without offering alternatives is referred to as retreatism.
Rebellion	A rebellion is, in the most general sense, a refusal to accept authority. It may therefore be seen as encompassing a range of behaviors from civil disobedience to a violent organized attempt to destroy established authority. It is often used in reference to armed resistance against an established government, but can also refer to mass nonviolent resistance movements.
Kuhn	Kuhn is most famous for his book The Structure of Scientific Revolutions (SSR) (1962) in which he presented the idea that science does not progress via a linear accumulation of new knowledge, but instead undergoes periodic revolutions which he calls "paradigm shifts", in which the nature of scientific inquiry within a particular field is abruptly transformed.
Mode	In statistics, mode means the most frequent value assumed by a random variable, or occurring in a sampling of a random variable.
Government	A government is a body that has the authority to make and the power to enforce laws within a civil, corporate, religious, academic, or other organization or group.
Normlessness	Emile Durkheim described anomie which is state of relative normlessness or a state in which norms have been eroded.
Durkheim	Durkheim sought to create one of the first scientific approaches to social phenomena. Along with Herbert Spencer, Durkheim was one of the first people to explain the existence and quality of different parts of a society by reference to what function they served in keeping the society healthy and balanced—a position that would come to be known as functionalism.
Anomie	Durkheim's designation for a condition in which social control becomes ineffective as a result of the loss of shared values and a sense of purpose in society is defined as anomie.
Mean	In statistics, mean has two related meanings: a)the average in ordinary English, which is also called the arithmetic mean (and is distinguished from the geometric mean or harmonic mean). The average is also called sample mean. b)the expected value of a random variable, which is also called the population mean.
Stereotype	A stereotype refers to widely shared beliefs about the characteristic traits, attitudes, and behaviors of members of various social groups, including the assumption that the members of such groups are usually all alike.
Social class	A category of people who occupy a similar position in relation to the means through which goods and services are produced in a society is a social class.
Murder	Murder is the unlawful, premeditated killing of a human being by another. The penalty for murder is usually either life imprisonment, or in jurisdictions with capital punishment, the death penalty.
Minority group	A minority group or subordinate group is a sociological group that does not constitute a politically dominant plurality of the total population of a given society.
Social status	Social status refers to a position in a social relationship, a characteristic that locates individuals in relation to other people and sets of role expectations.

Working class	Working class refers to a social class of industrial societies broadly composed of people involved in manual occupation.
Downward mobility	Downward mobility refers to social mobility in which individuals' wealth, income, or status is lower than what they or their parents once had.
Social problem	A social condition that is perceived as having harmful effects is a social problem. Opinions about whether a condition is a social problem vary among groups and depend upon how and by whom the condition is defined and perceived in society.
Middle class	A social class broadly defined occupationally as those working in white-collar and lower managerial occupations and is sometimes defined by reference to income levels or subjective identification of the participants in the study are referred to as middle class.
Social network	A social network is a social structure made of nodes which are generally individuals or organizations. It indicates the ways in which they are connected through various social familiarities ranging from casual acquaintance to close familial bonds.
Upper class	Upper class refers to a social class roughly composed of the more affluent members of society, especially those who have great wealth, control over businesses or hold large numbers of stocks and shares.
Social support	Social support is the physical and emotional comfort given to us by our family, friends, co-workers and others. It is knowing that we are part of a community of people who love and care for us, and value and think well of us.
Marital status	A person's marital status describes their relationship with a significant other. Some common statuses are: married, single, separated, divorced, widowed, engaged, invalid, annulled, living common-law. The number of children may also be specified and, in this case, becomes synonymous with family status. For example: married with no children. Marital status is often a question on censuses, credit card applications, and many different polls.
Divorce rate	The number of divorces over a specified period per specified popularion.The divorce rate is often calculated per 1,000 population or by estimating the proportion of all marriages that are expected to end in divorce.
Census	A census is the process of obtaining information about every member of a population. It can be contrasted with sampling in which information is only obtained from a subset of a population. As such it is a method used for accumulating statistical data, and it is also vital to democracy.
Disability	A physical or health condition that stigmatizes or causes discrimination, is referred to as a disability.
Life expectancy	The number of years a newborn in a particular society can expect to live is referred to as a life expectancy.
Feminist movement	The collective activities of individuals, groups, and organizations whose goal is the fair and equal treatment of women and men around the world is a feminist movement. They campaign on issues such as reproductive rights (including abortion), domestic violence, maternity leave, equal pay, sexual harassment, and sexual violence.
Poverty line	The poverty threshold, or poverty line, is the level of income below which one cannot afford to purchase all the resources one requires to live. Thus, by definition, nobody lives below the poverty line.
Role theory	Role theory refers to a theory that explains hypnotic events in terms of the person's ability to act as though he or she were hypnotized. Role theory differs from faking in that subjects cooperate and focus on hypnotic suggestions instead of pretending to be hypnotized.

Ageism	Ageism refers to prejudice against a person on the grounds of age in the belief that the age category is inferior to other age categories and that unequal treatment is therefore justified.
Life chances	Life chances are the opportunities each individual has to improve their quality of life. The concept was introduced by German sociologist Max Weber. It is a probabilistic concept, describing how likely it is, given certain factors, that an individual's life will turn out a certain way.
Discourse	In the social sciences, a discourse is considered to be an institutionalized way of thinking, a social boundary defining what can be said about a specific topic.
Demography	Demography is the scientific study of human population dynamics. It encompasses the study of the size, structure and distribution of populations, and how populations change over time due to births, deaths, migration and ageing.
Late adulthood	The developmental period that lasts from about 60 to 70 years of age until death, is referred to as late adulthood.
Consciousness	The awareness of the senzations, thoughts, and feelings being experienced at a given moment is referred to as consciousness.
Social theory	Social theory refers to the use of theoretical frameworks to explain and analyze social patterns and large-scale social structures. Social theory attempts to answer the question 'what is?', not 'what should be?'. One should therefore not confuse it with philosophy or with belief.
Social psychology	Social psychology refers to the study of the effects of social environments on the psychological functioning of individuals.
Organization	In sociology organization is understood as planned, coordinated and purposeful action of human beings to construct or compile a common tangible or intangible product or service.

Minority group — A minority group or subordinate group is a sociological group that does not constitute a politically dominant plurality of the total population of a given society.

Dominant group — The opposite of minority group, that possesses more wealth, power, and prestige in a society is a dominant group.

Discrimination — Discrimination refers to the denial of equal access to social resources to people on the basis of their group membership.

Amish — The Amish have, on occasion, encountered discrimination and hostility from their neighbors. During the World Wars, Amish nonresistance sparked many incidents of harassment, and young Amish men forcibly inducted into the services in violation of the Thirteenth Amendment to the U.S. Constitution were subjected to various forms of ill-treatment.

Society — A society is a grouping of individuals, which is characterized by common interest and may have distinctive culture and institutions.

Subculture — A group within the broader society that has values, norms and lifestyle distinct from those of the majority, is referred to as a subculture.

Social class — A category of people who occupy a similar position in relation to the means through which goods and services are produced in a society is a social class.

Ethnic group — An ethnic group is a human population whose members identify with each other, usually on the basis of a presumed common genealogy or ancestry.

Double jeopardy — Double jeopardy (also called "autrefois acquit" meaning "already acquitted") is a procedural defense (and, in many countries such as the United States, Canada, and India, a constitutional right) that forbids a defendant from being tried a second time for a crime, after having already been tried for the same crime.

Life expectancy — The number of years a newborn in a particular society can expect to live is referred to as a life expectancy.

Census — A census is the process of obtaining information about every member of a population. It can be contrasted with sampling in which information is only obtained from a subset of a population. As such it is a method used for accumulating statistical data, and it is also vital to democracy.

Metropolitan area — A metropolitan area is a large population center consisting of a large city and its adjacent zone of influence, or of several neighboring cities or towns and adjoining areas, with one or more large cities serving as its hub or hubs.

Extended family — Extended family refers to a family group consisting of more than two generations of the same kinship line living either within the same household or, more usually in the west, very close to one another.

Community — Community refers to a group of people who share a common sense of identity and interact with one another on a sustained basis.

Immigration — Although human migration has existed for hundreds of thousands of years, immigration in the modern sense refers to movement of people from one nation-state to another, where they are not citizens.

Coping — Efforts to control, reduce, or learn to tolerate the threats that lead to stress is referred to as coping.

Acculturation — Acculturation refers to the voluntary adoption of the norms, values and lifestyle of the dominant culture. It is the exchange of cultural features which result when groups come into continuous firsthand contact.

Educational attainment	Educational attainment is a term commonly used by statisticans to refer to the highest degree of education an individual has completed.
Prestige	Prestige refers to social respect accorded to an individual or group because of the status of their position.
Baby Boomer	A baby boomer is someone who was born during the period of increased birth rates when economic prosperity rose in many countries following World War II. In the United States, the baby boomer term is commonly applied to people with birth years from the span 1946 to 1964, which may comprise more than one generation.
Labor force	Normally, the labor force consists of everyone of working age (typically above a certain age (around 14 to 16) and below retirement (around 65) who are participating workers, that is people actively employed or seeking employment.
Racism	Racism is a belief in the moral or biological superiority of one race or ethnic group over another or others.
Ageism	Ageism refers to prejudice against a person on the grounds of age in the belief that the age category is inferior to other age categories and that unequal treatment is therefore justified.
Median	The number that falls halfway in a range of numbers, or the score below which are half the scores and above which are the other half is a median.
Government	A government is a body that has the authority to make and the power to enforce laws within a civil, corporate, religious, academic, or other organization or group.
Chicano	Chicano is a cultural identity used primarily by people of Mexican descent in the United States. While its meaning has changed over time and varies regionally, it tends to refer to a Mexican American (usually second- or third-generation) who has a strong sense of ethnic identity and an accompanying political consciousness.
Social position	The social identity an individual has in a given group or society, where social positions may be general in nature or may be more specific, is referred to as a social position.
Social structure	The term social structure, used in a general sense, refers to entities or groups in definite relation to each other, to relatively enduring patterns of behavior and relationship within social systems, or to social institutions and norms becoming embedded into social systems in such a way that they shape the behavior of actors within those social systems.
Social group	A group that consists of two or more people who interact frequently and share a common identity and a feeling of interdependence, is referred to as a social group.
Neighborhood	A neighborhood is a geographically localized community located within a larger city, town or suburb. Traditionally, a neighborhood is small enough that the neighbors are all able to know each other.
Rationalization	Rationalization is the process whereby an increasing number of social actions and interactions become based on considerations of efficiency or calculation rather than on motivations derived from custom, tradition, or emotion.
Cultural diversity	Cultural diversity is the variety of human societies or cultures in a specific region, or in the world as a whole.
Assimilation	A minority group's internalization of the values and norms of the dominant culture is referred to as assimilation.
Mean	In statistics, mean has two related meanings: a)the average in ordinary English, which is also called the arithmetic mean (and is distinguished from the geometric mean or harmonic mean). The average is also called sample mean. b)the expected value of a random variable,

which is also called the population mean.

Amalgamation The combination of several cultures in a society to produce a new culture is referred to as amalgamation.

Gerontology Gerontology is the study of the elderly, and of the aging process itself.

Slavery Slavery refers to an extreme form of stratification in which some people are owned by others.

Ritual A ritual is a set of actions, performed mainly for their symbolic value, which is prescribed by a religion or by the traditions of a community.

Attitude Attitude refers to an enduring mental representation of a person, place, or thing that evokes an emotional response and related behavior.

Prejudice Prejudice is, as the name implies, the process of "pre-judging" something. It implies coming to a judgment on a subject before learning where the preponderance of evidence actually lies, or forming a judgment without direct experience.

Socioeconomic status An overall rank based on characteristics such as education and occupation, used to describe people's positions in stratification systems is referred to as socioeconomic status.

Relative deprivation Relative deprivation refers to a perceived disadvantage in social or economic standing based on a comparison to others in a society. It is a term used in social sciences to describe feelings or measures of economic, political, or social deprivation that are relative rather than absolute

Statistics Statistics is a mathematical science pertaining to the collection, analysis, interpretation, and presentation of data. It is applicable to a wide variety of academic disciplines, from the physical and social sciences to the humanities; it is also used and misused for making informed decisions in all areas of business and government.

Interdependence Interdependence is a dynamic of being mutually responsible to and sharing a common set of principles with others. This concept differs dinstinctly from "dependence" in that an interdependent relationship implies that all participants are emotionally, economically, and/or morally "independent."

Autonomy Autonomy is a concept found in moral, political, and bioethical philosophy. Within these contexts it refers to the capacity of a rational individual to make an informed, uncoerced decision. In moral and political philosophy, autonomy is often used as the basis for determining moral responsibility for one's actions.

Murder Murder is the unlawful, premeditated killing of a human being by another. The penalty for murder is usually either life imprisonment, or in jurisdictions with capital punishment, the death penalty.

Organization In sociology organization is understood as planned, coordinated and purposeful action of human beings to construct or compile a common tangible or intangible product or service.

Social change Social change refers to alteration in social structures or culture over time.

Cultural pluralism Cultural pluralism refers to the more or less peaceful coexistence of multiple subcultures within a given society.

Melting pot The melting pot is a metaphor for the way in which homogeneous societies develop, in which the ingredients in the pot (people of different cultures and religions) are combined so as to lose their discrete identities to some degree, yielding a final product which has a more uniform consistency and flavor, and which is quite different from the original inputs.

Pluralism Pluralism is, in the general sense, the affirmation and acceptance of diversity. Pluralism is connected with the hope that this process of conflict and dialogue will lead to a definition

and subsequent realization of the common good that is best for all members of society.

Ideology Ideology refers to shared ideas or beliefs which serve to justify and support the interests of a particular group or organizations.

Social problem A social condition that is perceived as having harmful effects is a social problem. Opinions about whether a condition is a social problem vary among groups and depend upon how and by whom the condition is defined and perceived in society.

American Dream The American Dream is a subjective term usually implying a successful and satisfying life. This term usually implies financial security and material comfort, but can also imply a dream of fame, exceeding social, ethnic, or class boundaries, or simply living a fulfilling life. Perceptions of the American dream are usually framed in terms of American capitalism, its associated meritocracy, and the freedoms guaranteed by the U.S. Bill of Rights.

Social issue Social issue refers to matters that can be explained only by factors outside an individual's control and immediate social environment. They usually concern more than a single individual and affect many individuals in a society.

Public health Public health is concerned with threats to the overall health of a community based on population health analysis.

Social forces Social forces are the typical basic drives, or motives, which lead to the fundamental types of association and group relationship.

Institutiona-ization The term institutionalization is widely used in social theory to denote the process of making something (for example a concept, a social role, particular values and norms, or modes of behavior) become embedded within an organization, social system, or society as an established custom or norm within that system.

Dementia A global term for any neurological disorder in which the primary symptoms involve a deterioration of mental functioning is defined as dementia.

Significant other	Significant other is a gender-blind, politically correct term to refer to a person's partner in an intimate relationship without disclosing or presuming anything about his or her marital status or sexual orientation.
Marital status	A person's marital status describes their relationship with a significant other. Some common statuses are: married, single, separated, divorced, widowed, engaged, invalid, annulled, living common-law. The number of children may also be specified and, in this case, becomes synonymous with family status. For example: married with no children. Marital status is often a question on censuses, credit card applications, and many different polls.
Norm	In sociology, a norm, or social norm, is a rule that is socially enforced. Social sanctioning is what distinguishes norms from other cultural products such as meaning and values.
Median	The number that falls halfway in a range of numbers, or the score below which are half the scores and above which are the other half is a median.
Community	Community refers to a group of people who share a common sense of identity and interact with one another on a sustained basis.
Organization	In sociology organization is understood as planned, coordinated and purposeful action of human beings to construct or compile a common tangible or intangible product or service.
Middle class	A social class broadly defined occupationally as those working in white-collar and lower managerial occupations and is sometimes defined by reference to income levels or subjective identification of the participants in the study are referred to as middle class.
Upper class	Upper class refers to a social class roughly composed of the more affluent members of society, especially those who have great wealth, control over businesses or hold large numbers of stocks and shares.
Symbolic interaction	Symbolic interaction refers to the use of symbols by people to present themselves to others and interpret one another's behavior.
Family life cycle	The phases, or stages, of the family life span, each of which is characterized by changes in family structure, composition, and functions, is referred to as a family life cycle.
Mean	In statistics, mean has two related meanings: a)the average in ordinary English, which is also called the arithmetic mean (and is distinguished from the geometric mean or harmonic mean). The average is also called sample mean. b)the expected value of a random variable, which is also called the population mean.
Social responsibility	Social responsibility is a doctrine that claims that an entity whether it is state, government, corporation, organization or individual has a responsibility to society. This responsibility can be "negative," in that it is a responsibility to refrain from acting, or it can be "positive," meaning a responsibility to act.
Ideal type	Weber's construct of a pure type, constructed by emphasizing logical or consistent traits is referred to as an ideal type.
Society	A society is a grouping of individuals, which is characterized by common interest and may have distinctive culture and institutions.
Longitudinal study	A type of developmental study in which the same group of participants is followed and measured at different ages is a longitudinal study.
Range	A measure of variability defined as the high score in a distribution minus the low score is referred to as a range.
Masculinity	Masculinity refers to the characteristic forms of behavior expected of men in any given culture.

Refractory period	Refractory period refers to a phase following firing during which a neuron is less sensitive to messages from other neurons and will not fire. In the sexual response cycle, a period of time following orgasm during which an individual is not responsive to sexual stimulation.
Marital adjustment	Marital adjustment refers to the process of modifying, adapting, and altering individual and couple patterns of behavior and interaction to achieve maximum satisfaction in a marriage.
Direct relationship	In mathematics and statistics, a positive or direct relationship is a relationship between two variables in which they both increase or decrease in conjunction.
Division of labor	Division of labor is the specialisation of cooperative labor in specific, circumscribed tasks and roles, intended to increase efficiency of output.
Nuclear family	The term nuclear family was developed in the western world to distinguish the family group consisting of parents and their children, usually a father, mother, and children, from what is known as an extended family.
Mass society	Mass society is a society in which the concerns of the majority – the lower and middle social classes – play a prominent role, characterized by extension of voting rights, an improved standard of living for the lower classes and mass education.
Labor force	Normally, the labor force consists of everyone of working age (typically above a certain age (around 14 to 16) and below retirement (around 65) who are participating workers, that is people actively employed or seeking employment.
Extended family	Extended family refers to a family group consisting of more than two generations of the same kinship line living either within the same household or, more usually in the west, very close to one another.
Propinquity	In social psychology, propinquity is one of the main factors leading to interpersonal attraction. It refers to the physical or psychological proximity between people. For example, two people living on the same floor of a building have a higher propinquity than those living on different floors.
Stereotype	A stereotype refers to widely shared beliefs about the characteristic traits, attitudes, and behaviors of members of various social groups, including the assumption that the members of such groups are usually all alike.
Social support	Social support is the physical and emotional comfort given to us by our family, friends, co-workers and others. It is knowing that we are part of a community of people who love and care for us, and value and think well of us.
Government	A government is a body that has the authority to make and the power to enforce laws within a civil, corporate, religious, academic, or other organization or group.
Cohort	A cohort is a group of subjects, most often humans from a given population, defined by experiencing an event (typically birth) in a particular time span.
Life expectancy	The number of years a newborn in a particular society can expect to live is referred to as a life expectancy.
Authority	Authority refers to power that is attached to a position that others perceive as legitimate.
Attitude	Attitude refers to an enduring mental representation of a person, place, or thing that evokes an emotional response and related behavior.
Anticipatory socialization	The process of learning how to perform a role attached to a status we do not yet occupy is referred to as anticipatory socialization.
Socialization	Socialization refers to the lifelong processes through which humans develop an awareness of social norms and values, and achieve a distinct sense of self.

Statistics	Statistics is a mathematical science pertaining to the collection, analysis, interpretation, and presentation of data. It is applicable to a wide variety of academic disciplines, from the physical and social sciences to the humanities; it is also used and misused for making informed decisions in all areas of business and government.
Social relation	Social relation can refer to a multitude of social interactions, regulated by social norms, between two or more people, with each having a social position and performing a social role.
Voluntary association	A voluntary association is a group of individuals who voluntarily enter into an agreement to form a body (or organization) to accomplish a purpose.
Adaptation	Adaptation refers to the ability of a sociocultural system to change with the demands of a changing physical or social environment.
Social isolation	A type of loneliness that occurs when a person lacks a sense of integrated involvement. Being deprived of participation in a group or community involving companionship, shared interests, organized activities, and meaningful roles causes a person to feel is a social isolation.
Depression	In the field of psychiatry, the word depression can also have this meaning of low mood but more specifically refers to a mental illness when it has reached a severity and duration to warrant a diagnosis, whether there is an obvious situational cause or not.
Sex ratio	Sex ratio is the ratio of males to females in a population. The primary sex ratio is the ratio at the time of conception, secondary sex ratio is the ratio at time of birth. In humans the secondary sex ratio is commonly assumed to be 105 boys to 100 girls. In human societies, however, sex ratios at birth or among infants may be considerably skewed by sex-selective abortion and infanticide.
Mortality rate	Mortality rate is a measure of the number of deaths in some population, scaled to the size of that population, per unit time. Mortality rate is typically expressed in units of deaths per 1000 individuals per year; thus, a mortality rate of 10000.5 in a population of 100,000 would mean 1,000,500 deaths per year in the entire population.
Polygyny	Polygyny refers to a form of marriage in which a man may have more than one wife at the same time.
Fictive kin	A friend who is assigned a kin relationship based on his or her exceptional participation in sharing exchanges of emotional support, goods, and services, thus meeting the dual expectations of friends and kin is referred to as fictive kin.
Social network	A social network is a social structure made of nodes which are generally individuals or organizations. It indicates the ways in which they are connected through various social familiarities ranging from casual acquaintance to close familial bonds.
Complex family	Complex Family is a generic term for any family structure involving more than two adults. The term can refer to any extended family or to a polygamy of any type. It is often used to refer to the group marriage form of polygamy.
Variable	A characteristic that varies in value or magnitude along which an object, individual or group may be categorized, such as income or age, is referred to as a variable.
Punishment	Punishment is the practice of imposing something unpleasant on a subject as a response to some unwanted behavior or disobedience that the subject has displayed.
Reinforcement	A stimulus that follows a response and increases the frequency of the response is a reinforcement.
Social structure	The term social structure, used in a general sense, refers to entities or groups in definite relation to each other, to relatively enduring patterns of behavior and relationship within social systems, or to social institutions and norms becoming embedded into social systems in

	such a way that they shape the behavior of actors within those social systems.
Sandwich generation	Middle-aged adults caught between care-giving for their children and for their elderly parents, are referred to as a sandwich generation.
Social issue	Social issue refers to matters that can be explained only by factors outside an individual's control and immediate social environment. They usually concern more than a single individual and affect many individuals in a society.
Public policy	Public policy is a course of action or inaction chosen by public authorities to address a problem. Public policy is expressed in the body of laws, regulations, decisions and actions of government.
Gerontology	Gerontology is the study of the elderly, and of the aging process itself.
Late adulthood	The developmental period that lasts from about 60 to 70 years of age until death, is referred to as late adulthood.
Gender	Gender refers to socially defined behavior regarded as appropriate for the members of each
Social problem	A social condition that is perceived as having harmful effects is a social problem. Opinions about whether a condition is a social problem vary among groups and depend upon how and by whom the condition is defined and perceived in society.
Social psychology	Social psychology refers to the study of the effects of social environments on the psychological functioning of individuals.
Industrial society	In sociology, industrial society refers to a society with a modern societal structure. Such a structure developed in the west in the period of time following the industrial revolution. They are generally mass societies,
Social behavior	Social behavior is behavior directed towards, or taking place between, members of the same species.

Adolescence	Adolescence is the transitional stage of human development in which a juvenile matures into an adult. This transition involves biological (i.e. pubertal), social, and psychological changes, though the biological ones are the easiest to measure objectively.
Mean	In statistics, mean has two related meanings: a)the average in ordinary English, which is also called the arithmetic mean (and is distinguished from the geometric mean or harmonic mean). The average is also called sample mean. b)the expected value of a random variable, which is also called the population mean.
Society	A society is a grouping of individuals, which is characterized by common interest and may have distinctive culture and institutions.
Social role	A social role is a set of connected behaviors, rights and obligations as conceptualized by actors in a social situation. It is mostly defined as an expected behavior in a given individual social status and social position.
Full employment	A situation in which everyone or nearly everyone who wants to work can find a job is full employment.
Anticipatory socialization	The process of learning how to perform a role attached to a status we do not yet occupy is referred to as anticipatory socialization.
Socialization	Socialization refers to the lifelong processes through which humans develop an awareness of social norms and values, and achieve a distinct sense of self.
Elite	The elite is a relatively small dominant group within a larger society, which enjoys a privileged status which is upheld by individuals of lower social status within the structure of a group.
Punishment	Punishment is the practice of imposing something unpleasant on a subject as a response to some unwanted behavior or disobedience that the subject has displayed.
Community	Community refers to a group of people who share a common sense of identity and interact with one another on a sustained basis.
Hierarchy	A hierarchy is a system of ranking and organizing things or people, where each element of the system (except for the top element) is subordinate to a single other element. A hierarchy can link entities either directly or indirectly, and either vertically or horizontally. The only direct links in a hierarchy are to one's immediate superior, or to one of one's subordinates.
Social class	A category of people who occupy a similar position in relation to the means through which goods and services are produced in a society is a social class.
Capitalism	Capitalism is an economic system in which the means of production are owned mostly privately, and capital is invested in the production, distribution and other trade of goods and services, for profit in a competitive free market.
Max Weber	Max Weber was a German political economist and sociologist who is considered one of the founders of the modern study of sociology and public administration. His major works deal with rationalisation in sociology of religion and government, but he also contributed much in the field of economics. His most famous work is his essay The Protestant Ethic and the Spirit of Capitalism, which began his work in the sociology of religion.
Industrial society	In sociology, industrial society refers to a society with a modern societal structure. Such a structure developed in the west in the period of time following the industrial revolution. They are generally mass societies,
Attitude	Attitude refers to an enduring mental representation of a person, place, or thing that evokes an emotional response and related behavior.

Cohort — A cohort is a group of subjects, most often humans from a given population, defined by experiencing an event (typically birth) in a particular time span.

Organization — In sociology organization is understood as planned, coordinated and purposeful action of human beings to construct or compile a common tangible or intangible product or service.

Prestige — Prestige refers to social respect accorded to an individual or group because of the status of their position.

Range — A measure of variability defined as the high score in a distribution minus the low score is referred to as a range.

Working class — Working class refers to a social class of industrial societies broadly composed of people involved in manual occupation.

Work motivation — Work motivation refers to the conditions and processes responsible for the arousal, direction, magnitude, and maintenance of effort one puts forth in one's job.

Labor force — Normally, the labor force consists of everyone of working age (typically above a certain age (around 14 to 16) and below retirement (around 65) who are participating workers, that is people actively employed or seeking employment.

Social status — Social status refers to a position in a social relationship, a characteristic that locates individuals in relation to other people and sets of role expectations.

Social interaction — Social interaction is a dynamic, changing sequence of social actions between individuals (or groups) who modify their actions and reactions due to the actions by their interaction partner(s). In other words they are events in which people attach meaning to a situation, interpret what others are meaning, and respond accordingly.

Role expectation — A term used to describe a group's or society's definition of the way a specific role ought to be played is referred to as a role expectation.

Berger — Berger is perhaps best known for his view that social reality is a form of consciousness. Central to his work is the relationship between society and the individual. In his book The Social Construction of Reality Berger develops a sociological theory: 'Society as Objective Reality and as Subjective Reality'. His analysis of society as subjective reality describes the process by which an individual's conception of reality is produced by his or her interaction with social structures.

Occupational prestige — Occupational prestige refers to the consensual nature of rating a job based on the collective belief of its worthiness.

Convention — A convention is a set of agreed, stipulated or generally accepted social norms, norms, standards or criteria, often taking the form of a custom.

Symbolic interaction — Symbolic interaction refers to the use of symbols by people to present themselves to others and interpret one another's behavior.

Compulsion — An apparently irresistible urge to repeat an act or engage in ritualistic behavior, often despite negative consequences is referred to as a compulsion.

Census — A census is the process of obtaining information about every member of a population. It can be contrasted with sampling in which information is only obtained from a subset of a population. As such it is a method used for accumulating statistical data, and it is also vital to democracy.

Statistics — Statistics is a mathematical science pertaining to the collection, analysis, interpretation, and presentation of data. It is applicable to a wide variety of academic disciplines, from the physical and social sciences to the humanities; it is also used and misused for making informed decisions in all areas of business and government.

Gender	Gender refers to socially defined behavior regarded as appropriate for the members of each
Institutiona-ization	The term institutionalization is widely used in social theory to denote the process of making something (for example a concept, a social role, particular values and norms, or modes of behavior) become embedded within an organization, social system, or society as an established custom or norm within that system.
Crude birthrate	Crude birthrate refers to a statistical measure representing the number of births within a given population per year, normally calculated in terms of the number of births per thousand members.
Bureaucracy	Bureaucracy refers to a formal organization marked by a clear hierarchy of authority, the existence of written rules of procedure, staffed by full-time salaried officials, and striving for the efficient attainment of organizational goals.
Government	A government is a body that has the authority to make and the power to enforce laws within a civil, corporate, religious, academic, or other organization or group.
Social skill	A social skill is a skill used to interact and communicate with others to assist status in the social structure and other motivations. Social rules and social relations are created, communicated, and changed in verbal and nonverbal ways creating social complexity useful in identifying outsiders and intelligent breeding partners.
Variable	A characteristic that varies in value or magnitude along which an object, individual or group may be categorized, such as income or age, is referred to as a variable.
Social structure	The term social structure, used in a general sense, refers to entities or groups in definite relation to each other, to relatively enduring patterns of behavior and relationship within social systems, or to social institutions and norms becoming embedded into social systems in such a way that they shape the behavior of actors within those social systems.
Social support	Social support is the physical and emotional comfort given to us by our family, friends, co-workers and others. It is knowing that we are part of a community of people who love and care for us, and value and think well of us.
Reference group	Individuals almost universally have a bond toward a Reference Group. These are groups to which the individual does not have real membership, but to which he conceptually relates him/herself, and from which he might accept goals and values as a part of his/her self identity.
Clique	A clique is an informal and restricted social group formed by people who share common interests. They are often subsets of larger social groups.
Norm	In sociology, a norm, or social norm, is a rule that is socially enforced. Social sanctioning is what distinguishes norms from other cultural products such as meaning and values.
Mortality rate	Mortality rate is a measure of the number of deaths in some population, scaled to the size of that population, per unit time. Mortality rate is typically expressed in units of deaths per 1000 individuals per year; thus, a mortality rate of 10000.5 in a population of 100,000 would mean 1,000,500 deaths per year in the entire population.
Depression	In the field of psychiatry, the word depression can also have this meaning of low mood but more specifically refers to a mental illness when it has reached a severity and duration to warrant a diagnosis, whether there is an obvious situational cause or not.
Anomie	Durkheim's designation for a condition in which social control becomes ineffective as a result of the loss of shared values and a sense of purpose in society is defined as anomie.
Significant other	Significant other is a gender-blind, politically correct term to refer to a person's partner in an intimate relationship without disclosing or presuming anything about his or her

	marital status or sexual orientation.
Social group	A group that consists of two or more people who interact frequently and share a common identity and a feeling of interdependence, is referred to as a social group.
Industrialization	Industrialization is a process of social and economic change whereby a human society is transformed from a pre-industrial (an economy where the amount of capital accumulated is low) to an industrial state
Child labor	Child labor is the employment of children under an age determined by law or custom. This practice is considered exploitative by many countries and international organizations. Child labor was not seen as a problem throughout most of history, only becoming a disputed issue with the beginning of universal schooling and the concepts of laborers and children's rights.
Discrimination	Discrimination refers to the denial of equal access to social resources to people on the basis of their group membership.
Civil rights	Civil rights are the protections and privileges of personal liberty given to all citizens by law. Civil rights are rights that are bestowed by nations on those within their territorial boundaries.
Technology	The application of logic, reason and knowledge to the problems of exploiting raw materials from the environment, is referred to as a technology.
Minority group	A minority group or subordinate group is a sociological group that does not constitute a politically dominant plurality of the total population of a given society.
Baby Boomer	A baby boomer is someone who was born during the period of increased birth rates when economic prosperity rose in many countries following World War II. In the United States, the baby boomer term is commonly applied to people with birth years from the span 1946 to 1964, which may comprise more than one generation.
Social problem	A social condition that is perceived as having harmful effects is a social problem. Opinions about whether a condition is a social problem vary among groups and depend upon how and by whom the condition is defined and perceived in society.
Parsons	Parsons was an advocate of "grand theory," an attempt to integrate all the social sciences into an overarching theoretical framework. His early work — The Structure of Social Action —reviewed the output of his great predecessors, especially Max Weber, Vilfredo Pareto, and Émile Durkheim, and attempted to derive from them a single "action theory" based on the assumptions that human action is voluntary, intentional, and symbolic.
Division of labor	Division of labor is the specialisation of cooperative labor in specific, circumscribed tasks and roles, intended to increase efficiency of output.
Durkheim	Durkheim sought to create one of the first scientific approaches to social phenomena. Along with Herbert Spencer, Durkheim was one of the first people to explain the existence and quality of different parts of a society by reference to what function they served in keeping the society healthy and balanced—a position that would come to be known as functionalism.
Gerontology	Gerontology is the study of the elderly, and of the aging process itself.
Multivariate analysis	The analysis of the simultaneous relationships among several variables is referred to as multivariate analysis. Examining simultaneously the effects of age, gender and social class on religiosity would be an example of multivariate analysis.
Paradigm	In social science, paradigm is used to describe the set of experiences, beliefs and values that affect the way an individual perceives reality and responds to that perception.
Social	Social psychology refers to the study of the effects of social environments on the

psychology	psychological functioning of individuals.
Merton	Merton coined the phrase "self-fulfilling prophecy." He also coined many other phrases that have gone into everyday use, such as "role model" and "unintended consequences".
Industrial sociology	Industrial sociology is both a study of the interaction of people within industry (e.g. boss-subordinate, inter-departmental, and management-union relations) and, on a macrosociological scale, the study of the impact of industrialization on whole societies.
Longitudinal study	A type of developmental study in which the same group of participants is followed and measured at different ages is a longitudinal study.
Demographics	The analysis of data used by advertizing agencies to target an audience by sex, age, income level, marital status, geographic location, and occupation are referred to as demographics.
Professional-zation	The social process through which an occupation acquires the cultural and structural characteristics of a profession is professionalization.
Mills	Mills is best remembered for studying the structure of Power in the U.S. in his book, The Power Elite. Mills was concerned with the responsibilities of intellectuals in post-World War II society, and advocated relevance and engagement over disinterested academic observation, as a "public intelligence apparatus" in challenging the crackpot policies of these institutional elite in the "Big Three", the economic, political and military.

Neighborhood	A neighborhood is a geographically localized community located within a larger city, town or suburb. Traditionally, a neighborhood is small enough that the neighbors are all able to know each other.
Community	Community refers to a group of people who share a common sense of identity and interact with one another on a sustained basis.
Range	A measure of variability defined as the high score in a distribution minus the low score is referred to as a range.
Fromm	Fromm's most well-known work, Escape from Freedom, focuses on the human urge to seek a source of authority and control upon reaching a freedom that was thought to be an individual's true desire. The culmination of Fromm's social and political philosophy was his book The Sane Society, published in 1955, which argued in favor of humanistic and democratic socialism. Building primarily upon the early works of Karl Marx, Fromm sought to re-emphasise the ideal of personal freedom, missing from most Soviet Marxism, and more frequently found in the writings of libertarian socialists and liberal theoreticians.
Mean	In statistics, mean has two related meanings: a)the average in ordinary English, which is also called the arithmetic mean (and is distinguished from the geometric mean or harmonic mean). The average is also called sample mean. b)the expected value of a random variable, which is also called the population mean.
Social status	Social status refers to a position in a social relationship, a characteristic that locates individuals in relation to other people and sets of role expectations.
Social order	Social order refers to a set of linked social structures, social institutions and social practices which conserve, maintain and enforce "normal" ways of relating and behaving.
Organization	In sociology organization is understood as planned, coordinated and purposeful action of human beings to construct or compile a common tangible or intangible product or service.
Social class	A category of people who occupy a similar position in relation to the means through which goods and services are produced in a society is a social class.
Status group	The sociologist Max Weber formulated a three-component theory of stratification in which he defines status group (also known as a status class) as a group of people (part of a society) that can be differentiated on the basis of non-economical qualities like honour, prestige and religion.
Coleman	Coleman was a sociological theorist, who studied the sociology of education, public policy, and was one of the earliest users of the term "social capital". His Foundations of Social Theory stands as one of the most important sociological contributions of the late-20th century.
Variable	A characteristic that varies in value or magnitude along which an object, individual or group may be categorized, such as income or age, is referred to as a variable.
Society	A society is a grouping of individuals, which is characterized by common interest and may have distinctive culture and institutions.
Hierarchy	A hierarchy is a system of ranking and organizing things or people, where each element of the system (except for the top element) is subordinate to a single other element. A hierarchy can link entities either directly or indirectly, and either vertically or horizontally. The only direct links in a hierarchy are to one's immediate superior, or to one of one's subordinates.
Social structure	The term social structure, used in a general sense, refers to entities or groups in definite relation to each other, to relatively enduring patterns of behavior and relationship within social systems, or to social institutions and norms becoming embedded into social systems in

	such a way that they shape the behavior of actors within those social systems.
Validity	The degree to which a measurement instrument measures what it is intended to measure is referred to as validity.
Social interaction	Social interaction is a dynamic, changing sequence of social actions between individuals (or groups) who modify their actions and reactions due to the actions by their interaction partner(s). In other words they are events in which people attach meaning to a situation, interpret what others are meaning, and respond accordingly.
Population density	Population density refers to the number of people per unit of area or unit volume.
Migration	The movement of people from one country or region to another in order to settle permanently, is referred to as a migration.
Metropolitan area	A metropolitan area is a large population center consisting of a large city and its adjacent zone of influence, or of several neighboring cities or towns and adjoining areas, with one or more large cities serving as its hub or hubs.
Cultural diversity	Cultural diversity is the variety of human societies or cultures in a specific region, or in the world as a whole.
Government	A government is a body that has the authority to make and the power to enforce laws within a civil, corporate, religious, academic, or other organization or group.
Social justice	Social justice refers to conceptions of justice applied to an entire society. It is based on the idea of a just society, which gives individuals and groups fair treatment and a just share of the benefits of society.
Social group	A group that consists of two or more people who interact frequently and share a common identity and a feeling of interdependence, is referred to as a social group.
Disability	A physical or health condition that stigmatizes or causes discrimination, is referred to as a disability.
Social issue	Social issue refers to matters that can be explained only by factors outside an individual's control and immediate social environment. They usually concern more than a single individual and affect many individuals in a society.
Social contact	Social contact is a pair of social actions with no further consequence - i.e. it is not likely to be repeated. It can sometimes be described as an accidental social interaction.
Crime	Crime refers to any action that violates criminal laws established by political authority. A crime in a nontechnical sense is an act that violates a very important political or moral command.
Census	A census is the process of obtaining information about every member of a population. It can be contrasted with sampling in which information is only obtained from a subset of a population. As such it is a method used for accumulating statistical data, and it is also vital to democracy.
Discrimination	Discrimination refers to the denial of equal access to social resources to people on the basis of their group membership.
Primary group	A primary group is a typically small social group whose members share close, personal, enduring primary relationships. These groups are marked by member's concern for one another, shared activities and culture, and long periods of time spent together.
Middle class	A social class broadly defined occupationally as those working in white-collar and lower managerial occupations and is sometimes defined by reference to income levels or subjective

identification of the participants in the study are referred to as middle class.

Working class Working class refers to a social class of industrial societies broadly composed of people involved in manual occupation.

Frequency In statistics the frequency of an event i is the number n_i of times the event occurred in the experiment or the study.

Marital status A person's marital status describes their relationship with a significant other. Some common statuses are: married, single, separated, divorced, widowed, engaged, invalid, annulled, living common-law. The number of children may also be specified and, in this case, becomes synonymous with family status. For example: married with no children. Marital status is often a question on censuses, credit card applications, and many different polls.

Institutiona-ization The term institutionalization is widely used in social theory to denote the process of making something (for example a concept, a social role, particular values and norms, or modes of behavior) become embedded within an organization, social system, or society as an established custom or norm within that system.

Total institution Total institution as defined by Erving Goffman, is an institution where all the aspects of life of individuals under the institution is controlled and regulated by the authorities of the organization. Total institutions are a social microcosmos dictated by hegemony and clear hierarchy.

Mental hospital A medical institution specializing in providing inpatient care for psychological disorders is a psychiatric hospital or mental hospital.

Goffman Goffman was one of the most influential sociologists of the twentieth century, on a par with Weber, Durkheim, Marx, and Mead, in whose footsteps he followed in developing a sociological social psychology. His greatest contribution to social theory is his formulation of symbolic interaction in his 1959 book The Presentation of Self in Everyday Life.

Depersonaliz-tion Depersonalization refers to the perceptual experience of one's body or surroundings becoming distorted or unreal.

Caste Caste refers to a closed form of stratification in which an individual's status is determined by birth and cannot be changed.

Ideal type Weber's construct of a pure type, constructed by emphasizing logical or consistent traits is referred to as an ideal type.

Centralization Centralization is the process by which the activities of an organization, particularly those regarding decision-making, become concentrated within a particular location and/or group.

Authority Authority refers to power that is attached to a position that others perceive as legitimate.

Attitude Attitude refers to an enduring mental representation of a person, place, or thing that evokes an emotional response and related behavior.

Decentralization Decentralization refers to the movement of people, jobs and activities from the center or core of major metropolitan areas to suburban and outlying locations.

Alienation In sociology and critical social theory, alienation refers to the individual's estrangement from traditional community and others in general.

Social distance Social distance describes the distance between different groups of society and is opposed to locational distance. The notion includes all differences such as social class, race/ethnicity or sexuality, but also the fact that the different groups do not mix. The term is often applied in cities, but its use is not limited to that.

Late adulthood The developmental period that lasts from about 60 to 70 years of age until death, is referred

	to as late adulthood.
Social forces	Social forces are the typical basic drives, or motives, which lead to the fundamental types of association and group relationship.
Prestige	Prestige refers to social respect accorded to an individual or group because of the status of their position.
Social ecology	The entire network of interactions and interdependencies among people, institutions, and cultural constructs to which the developing person must adapt psychologically is a social ecology.
Gerontology	Gerontology is the study of the elderly, and of the aging process itself.
Parsons	Parsons was an advocate of "grand theory," an attempt to integrate all the social sciences into an overarching theoretical framework. His early work — The Structure of Social Action —reviewed the output of his great predecessors, especially Max Weber, Vilfredo Pareto, and Émile Durkheim, and attempted to derive from them a single "action theory" based on the assumptions that human action is voluntary, intentional, and symbolic.
Paradigm	In social science, paradigm is used to describe the set of experiences, beliefs and values that affect the way an individual perceives reality and responds to that perception.
Modernization	The process of general social change brought about by the transition from an agrarian to an industrial mode of production, is referred to as modernization.
Depression	In the field of psychiatry, the word depression can also have this meaning of low mood but more specifically refers to a mental illness when it has reached a severity and duration to warrant a diagnosis, whether there is an obvious situational cause or not.

Coping	Efforts to control, reduce, or learn to tolerate the threats that lead to stress is referred to as coping.
Mean	In statistics, mean has two related meanings: a)the average in ordinary English, which is also called the arithmetic mean (and is distinguished from the geometric mean or harmonic mean). The average is also called sample mean. b)the expected value of a random variable, which is also called the population mean.
Social group	A group that consists of two or more people who interact frequently and share a common identity and a feeling of interdependence, is referred to as a social group.
Society	A society is a grouping of individuals, which is characterized by common interest and may have distinctive culture and institutions.
Social structure	The term social structure, used in a general sense, refers to entities or groups in definite relation to each other, to relatively enduring patterns of behavior and relationship within social systems, or to social institutions and norms becoming embedded into social systems in such a way that they shape the behavior of actors within those social systems.
Social order	Social order refers to a set of linked social structures, social institutions and social practices which conserve, maintain and enforce "normal" ways of relating and behaving.
Ritual	A ritual is a set of actions, performed mainly for their symbolic value, which is prescribed by a religion or by the traditions of a community.
Max Weber	Max Weber was a German political economist and sociologist who is considered one of the founders of the modern study of sociology and public administration. His major works deal with rationalisation in sociology of religion and government, but he also contributed much in the field of economics. His most famous work is his essay The Protestant Ethic and the Spirit of Capitalism, which began his work in the sociology of religion.
Bureaucracy	Bureaucracy refers to a formal organization marked by a clear hierarchy of authority, the existence of written rules of procedure, staffed by full-time salaried officials, and striving for the efficient attainment of organizational goals.
Frequency	In statistics the frequency of an event i is the number n_i of times the event occurred in the experiment or the study.
Extended family	Extended family refers to a family group consisting of more than two generations of the same kinship line living either within the same household or, more usually in the west, very close to one another.
Industrial society	In sociology, industrial society refers to a society with a modern societal structure. Such a structure developed in the west in the period of time following the industrial revolution. They are generally mass societies,
Attitude	Attitude refers to an enduring mental representation of a person, place, or thing that evokes an emotional response and related behavior.
Malinowski	Malinowski was a Polish anthropologist widely considered to be one of the most important anthropologists of the twentieth century because of his pioneering work on ethnographic fieldwork, the study of reciprocity, and his detailed contribution to the study of Melanesia.
Punishment	Punishment is the practice of imposing something unpleasant on a subject as a response to some unwanted behavior or disobedience that the subject has displayed.
Positive relationship	A statistical relationship in which high scores on one variable are related to high scores on another variable, is referred to as a direct or positive relationship.
Rationalization	Rationalization is the process whereby an increasing number of social actions and interactions become based on considerations of efficiency or calculation rather than on

	motivations derived from custom, tradition, or emotion.
Negative relationship	A relationship in which high scores on one variable are related to low scores on another is a negative relationship.
Community	Community refers to a group of people who share a common sense of identity and interact with one another on a sustained basis.
Berger	Berger is perhaps best known for his view that social reality is a form of consciousness. Central to his work is the relationship between society and the individual. In his book The Social Construction of Reality Berger develops a sociological theory: 'Society as Objective Reality and as Subjective Reality'. His analysis of society as subjective reality describes the process by which an individual's conception of reality is produced by his or her interaction with social structures.
Significant other	Significant other is a gender-blind, politically correct term to refer to a person's partner in an intimate relationship without disclosing or presuming anything about his or her marital status or sexual orientation.
Murder	Murder is the unlawful, premeditated killing of a human being by another. The penalty for murder is usually either life imprisonment, or in jurisdictions with capital punishment, the death penalty.
Euthanasia	The act of painlessly ending the lives of persons who are suffering from incurable diseases or severe disabilities, sometimes called mercy killing, is referred to as euthanasia.
Technology	The application of logic, reason and knowledge to the problems of exploiting raw materials from the environment, is referred to as a technology.
Consciousness	The awareness of the senzations, thoughts, and feelings being experienced at a given moment is referred to as consciousness.
Authority	Authority refers to power that is attached to a position that others perceive as legitimate.
Brain death	Brain death is defined as a complete and irreversible ceszation of brain activity. Absence of apparent brain function is not enough. Evidence of irreversibility is also required. Brain death is often confused with the state of vegetation.
Abortion	An abortion is the removal or expulsion of an embryo or fetus from the uterus, resulting in, or caused by, its death. This can occur spontaneously as a miscarriage, or be artificially induced through chemical, surgical or other means. Commonly, " abortion " refers to an induced procedure at any point in the pregnancy; medically, it is defined as a miscarriage or induced termination before twenty weeks gestation, which is considered nonviable.
Hospice	A health care facility designed to counsel and care for the terminally ill is a hospice.
Public opinion	Public opinion is the aggregate of individual attitudes or beliefs held by the adult population.
Intake	Intake refers to process during which a juvenile referral is received and a decision is made to file a petition in juvenile court to release the juvenile, to place the juvenile under supervision, or to refer the juvenile elsewhere.
Social isolation	A type of loneliness that occurs when a person lacks a sense of integrated involvement. Being deprived of participation in a group or community involving companionship, shared interests, organized activities, and meaningful roles causes a person to feel is a social isolation.
Social environment	The social environment is the direct influence of a group of individuals and their contributions to this environment, as both groups and individuals who are in frequent communication with each other within their cultural or socio-economical strata, which create role identity(-ies) and guide the individual's self (sociology) growth and their

	progression towards maturity.
Social network	A social network is a social structure made of nodes which are generally individuals or organizations. It indicates the ways in which they are connected through various social familiarities ranging from casual acquaintance to close familial bonds.
Social support	Social support is the physical and emotional comfort given to us by our family, friends, co-workers and others. It is knowing that we are part of a community of people who love and care for us, and value and think well of us.
Socialization	Socialization refers to the lifelong processes through which humans develop an awareness of social norms and values, and achieve a distinct sense of self.
Social psychology	Social psychology refers to the study of the effects of social environments on the psychological functioning of individuals.
Gerontology	Gerontology is the study of the elderly, and of the aging process itself.
Social construction of reality	The process by which our perception of reality is shaped largely by the subjective meaning that we give to an experience is a social construction of reality.
Sociology of knowledge	The sociology of knowledge is the study of the social origins of ideas, and of the effects prevailing ideas have on societies.
Social construction	A social construction is an institutionalized entity or artifact in a social system 'invented' or 'constructed' by participants in a particular culture or society that exists solely because people agree to behave as if it exists, or agree to follow certain conventional rules.
Strauss	Strauss was an American sociologist, who worked the field of medical sociology. Strauss is best known for his work on the methodology in qualitative research and in particular for the development of grounded theory, a general methodology he established together with Barney Glaser in the 1960s.
Glaser	Glaser, American sociologist and one of the founders of the grounded theory methodology. In 1999 Glaser founded the non-profit web based organization Grounded Theory Institute.
Adaptation	Adaptation refers to the ability of a sociocultural system to change with the demands of a changing physical or social environment.
Social issue	Social issue refers to matters that can be explained only by factors outside an individual's control and immediate social environment. They usually concern more than a single individual and affect many individuals in a society.
Religiosity	Religiosity refers to a sociological concept referring to the importance of religion in individuals lives.
Organization	In sociology organization is understood as planned, coordinated and purposeful action of human beings to construct or compile a common tangible or intangible product or service.

Variable	A characteristic that varies in value or magnitude along which an object, individual or group may be categorized, such as income or age, is referred to as a variable.
Range	A measure of variability defined as the high score in a distribution minus the low score is referred to as a range.
Mean	In statistics, mean has two related meanings: a)the average in ordinary English, which is also called the arithmetic mean (and is distinguished from the geometric mean or harmonic mean). The average is also called sample mean. b)the expected value of a random variable, which is also called the population mean.
Census	A census is the process of obtaining information about every member of a population. It can be contrasted with sampling in which information is only obtained from a subset of a population. As such it is a method used for accumulating statistical data, and it is also vital to democracy.
Median	The number that falls halfway in a range of numbers, or the score below which are half the scores and above which are the other half is a median.
Statistics	Statistics is a mathematical science pertaining to the collection, analysis, interpretation, and presentation of data. It is applicable to a wide variety of academic disciplines, from the physical and social sciences to the humanities; it is also used and misused for making informed decisions in all areas of business and government.
Government	A government is a body that has the authority to make and the power to enforce laws within a civil, corporate, religious, academic, or other organization or group.
Community	Community refers to a group of people who share a common sense of identity and interact with one another on a sustained basis.
Fear of crime	The fear of crime refers to the fear of being a victim of crime. Usually the fear is disproportionate to the likihood of being a victim of crime. Moral panics are often the cause of the rizing fear of crime.
Crime	Crime refers to any action that violates criminal laws established by political authority. A crime in a nontechnical sense is an act that violates a very important political or moral command.
Discrimination	Discrimination refers to the denial of equal access to social resources to people on the basis of their group membership.
Poverty line	The poverty threshold, or poverty line, is the level of income below which one cannot afford to purchase all the resources one requires to live. Thus, by definition, nobody lives below the poverty line.
Labor force	Normally, the labor force consists of everyone of working age (typically above a certain age (around 14 to 16) and below retirement (around 65) who are participating workers, that is people actively employed or seeking employment.
Society	A society is a grouping of individuals, which is characterized by common interest and may have distinctive culture and institutions.

Crime	Crime refers to any action that violates criminal laws established by political authority. A crime in a nontechnical sense is an act that violates a very important political or moral command.
Fear of crime	The fear of crime refers to the fear of being a victim of crime. Usually the fear is disproportionate to the likihood of being a victim of crime. Moral panics are often the cause of the rizing fear of crime.
Statistics	Statistics is a mathematical science pertaining to the collection, analysis, interpretation, and presentation of data. It is applicable to a wide variety of academic disciplines, from the physical and social sciences to the humanities; it is also used and misused for making informed decisions in all areas of business and government.
Aggravated Assault	Aggravated assault refers to an unlawful attack by one person upon another for the purpose of inflicting severe or aggravated bodily injury.
Robbery	The unlawful taking of, or the attempt to take something of value from another person or persons by using violence or the threat of violence, is referred to as a robbery.
Community	Community refers to a group of people who share a common sense of identity and interact with one another on a sustained basis.
Neighborhood	A neighborhood is a geographically localized community located within a larger city, town or suburb. Traditionally, a neighborhood is small enough that the neighbors are all able to know each other.
Larceny	Larceny is the trespassory taking and asportation of the (tangible) personal property of another with the intent to deprive him or her of it permanently.
Exploitation	In political economy, economics, and sociology, exploitation involves a persistent social relationship in which certain persons are being mistreated or unfairly used for the benefit of others. This corresponds to one ethical conception of exploitation, that is, the treatment of human beings as mere means to an end — or as mere "objects".
Sector	Sector refers to parts of the economy as judged by the economic activity that they constitute. For example agriculture, forestry, fishing and mining constitute the primary sector.
Public sector	Public sector refers to that part of a national economy subject to direct government ownership and control. The constituents of the public sector are the departments of central and local government, various government agencies and the nationalized industries.
Elder abuse	Elder abuse refers to a term used to describe physical abuse, psychological abuse, financial exploitation, and medical abuse or neglect of people age 65 or older.
Punishment	Punishment is the practice of imposing something unpleasant on a subject as a response to some unwanted behavior or disobedience that the subject has displayed.
Cycle of violence	The term cycle of violence refers to repeated acts of violence between groups as a cyclical pattern, associated with high emotions and doctrines retribution, revenge, such as "an eye for an eye."
Society	A society is a grouping of individuals, which is characterized by common interest and may have distinctive culture and institutions.
Positive relationship	A statistical relationship in which high scores on one variable are related to high scores on another variable, is referred to as a direct or positive relationship.
Child abuse	Child abuse refers to not only physical assaults on a child but also malnourishment, abandonment, neglect, emotional abuse and sexual abuse.

Social isolation	A type of loneliness that occurs when a person lacks a sense of integrated involvement. Being deprived of participation in a group or community involving companionship, shared interests, organized activities, and meaningful roles causes a person to feel is a social isolation.
Control group	A group of people in an experiment who are not exposed to the experimental stimulus under study are referred to as a control group.
Murder	Murder is the unlawful, premeditated killing of a human being by another. The penalty for murder is usually either life imprisonment, or in jurisdictions with capital punishment, the death penalty.
House arrest	House arrest refers to an offender is required to stay at home during specific periods of time; monitoring is done by random phone calls and visits or by electronic devices.
Public opinion	Public opinion is the aggregate of individual attitudes or beliefs held by the adult population.
Gerontology	Gerontology is the study of the elderly, and of the aging process itself.
Wright	Wright is an American sociologist. His work is concerned mainly with the study of social classes, and in particular with the task of providing an update to the Marxist concept of class. Wright has stressed the importance of the control of the means of production in defining 'class', while at the same trying to account for the situation of skilled employees, taking inspiration from Weberian accounts of authority.
Ageism	Ageism refers to prejudice against a person on the grounds of age in the belief that the age category is inferior to other age categories and that unequal treatment is therefore justified.
Criminology	Criminology refers to the systematic study of crime and the criminal justice system, including the police, courts, and prisons.
Variable	A characteristic that varies in value or magnitude along which an object, individual or group may be categorized, such as income or age, is referred to as a variable.
Rebellion	A rebellion is, in the most general sense, a refusal to accept authority. It may therefore be seen as encompassing a range of behaviors from civil disobedience to a violent organized attempt to destroy established authority. It is often used in reference to armed resistance against an established government, but can also refer to mass nonviolent resistance movements.
Criminal justice	Criminal justice refers to the system used by government to maintain social control, enforce laws, and administer justice. Law enforcement (police), courts, and corrections are the primary agencies charged with these responsibilities.

Crude birthrate	Crude birthrate refers to a statistical measure representing the number of births within a given population per year, normally calculated in terms of the number of births per thousand members.
Government	A government is a body that has the authority to make and the power to enforce laws within a civil, corporate, religious, academic, or other organization or group.
Community	Community refers to a group of people who share a common sense of identity and interact with one another on a sustained basis.
Disability	A physical or health condition that stigmatizes or causes discrimination, is referred to as a disability.
Cohort	A cohort is a group of subjects, most often humans from a given population, defined by experiencing an event (typically birth) in a particular time span.
Disengagement theory	Disengagement theory refers to the proposition that older persons make a normal and healthy adjustment to aging when they detach themselves from their social roles and prepare for their eventual death.
Contradiction	Marx's term to refer to mutually antagonistic tendencies within institutions or the broader society such as those between profit and competition within capitalism is referred to as a contradiction.
Society	A society is a grouping of individuals, which is characterized by common interest and may have distinctive culture and institutions.
Reference group	Individuals almost universally have a bond toward a Reference Group. These are groups to which the individual does not have real membership, but to which he conceptually relates him/herself, and from which he might accept goals and values as a part of his/her self identity.
Social group	A group that consists of two or more people who interact frequently and share a common identity and a feeling of interdependence, is referred to as a social group.
Attitude	Attitude refers to an enduring mental representation of a person, place, or thing that evokes an emotional response and related behavior.
Vested interest	An expectation of private gain that often underlies the expressed interest in a public issue is a vested interest.
Social movement	A social movement refers to large informal groupings of individuals and/or organizations focused on specific political or social issues, in other words, on carrying out, resisting or undoing a social change.
Interest group	Interest group refers to an organization that attempts to affect political decisions by supporting candidates sympathetic to their interests and by influencing those already in positions of authority.
Kuhn	Kuhn is most famous for his book The Structure of Scientific Revolutions (SSR) (1962) in which he presented the idea that science does not progress via a linear accumulation of new knowledge, but instead undergoes periodic revolutions which he calls "paradigm shifts", in which the nature of scientific inquiry within a particular field is abruptly transformed.
Coalition	A coalition is an alliance among entities, during which they cooperate in joint action, each in their own self-interest. This alliance may be temporary or a matter of convenience.
Consciousness	The awareness of the senzations, thoughts, and feelings being experienced at a given moment is referred to as consciousness.
Social change	Social change refers to alteration in social structures or culture over time.

Civil Rights Movement	Historically, the civil rights movement was a concentrated period of time around the world of approximately one generation (1954-1980) wherein there was much worldwide civil unrest and popular rebellion.
Civil rights	Civil rights are the protections and privileges of personal liberty given to all citizens by law. Civil rights are rights that are bestowed by nations on those within their territorial boundaries.
Discrimination	Discrimination refers to the denial of equal access to social resources to people on the basis of their group membership.
Organization	In sociology organization is understood as planned, coordinated and purposeful action of human beings to construct or compile a common tangible or intangible product or service.
Dependency ratio	Dependency ratio refers to the ratio of people of dependent ages to people of economically active ages.
Variable	A characteristic that varies in value or magnitude along which an object, individual or group may be categorized, such as income or age, is referred to as a variable.
Consensus	Agreement on basic social values by the members of a group or society is referred to as a consensus.
Range	A measure of variability defined as the high score in a distribution minus the low score is referred to as a range.
Welfare state	A government system which provides a range of human services for its citizens is referred to as a welfare state.
Labor force	Normally, the labor force consists of everyone of working age (typically above a certain age (around 14 to 16) and below retirement (around 65) who are participating workers, that is people actively employed or seeking employment.
Public opinion	Public opinion is the aggregate of individual attitudes or beliefs held by the adult population.
Social class	A category of people who occupy a similar position in relation to the means through which goods and services are produced in a society is a social class.
Working class	Working class refers to a social class of industrial societies broadly composed of people involved in manual occupation.
Unemployment rate	In economics, one who is willing to work at a prevailing wage rate yet is unable to find a paying job is considered to be unemployed. The unemployment rate is the number of unemployed workers divided by the total civilian labor force, which includes both the unemployed and those with jobs (all those willing and able to work for pay).
Status inconsistency	Status inconsistency is a situation where an individual's social positions have both positive and negative influences on his social status.
Hierarchy	A hierarchy is a system of ranking and organizing things or people, where each element of the system (except for the top element) is subordinate to a single other element. A hierarchy can link entities either directly or indirectly, and either vertically or horizontally. The only direct links in a hierarchy are to one's immediate superior, or to one of one's subordinates.
Ascribed status	Ascribed status is a social status a person is given from birth or assumes involuntarily later in life. For example, a person born into a wealthy family has a high ascribed status.
Socioeconomic status	An overall rank based on characteristics such as education and occupation, used to describe people's positions in stratification systems is referred to as socioeconomic status.

Achieved Status	Achieved status is a sociological term denoting a social position that a person assumes voluntarily which reflects personal skills, abilities, and efforts.
Social order	Social order refers to a set of linked social structures, social institutions and social practices which conserve, maintain and enforce "normal" ways of relating and behaving.
Full employment	A situation in which everyone or nearly everyone who wants to work can find a job is full employment.
Liberalism	Liberalism is an ideology, philosophical view, and political tradition which holds that liberty is the primary political value. Liberalism has its roots in the Western Age of Enlightenment.
Gerontocracy	A gerontocracy is a form of oligarchical rule in which an entity is ruled by leaders who are significantly older than most of the adult population. Often the political structure is such that political power within the ruling class accumulates with age, so that the oldest hold the most power.
Ideology	Ideology refers to shared ideas or beliefs which serve to justify and support the interests of a particular group or organizations.
Baby Boomer	A baby boomer is someone who was born during the period of increased birth rates when economic prosperity rose in many countries following World War II. In the United States, the baby boomer term is commonly applied to people with birth years from the span 1946 to 1964, which may comprise more than one generation.
Gerontology	Gerontology is the study of the elderly, and of the aging process itself.
Social issue	Social issue refers to matters that can be explained only by factors outside an individual's control and immediate social environment. They usually concern more than a single individual and affect many individuals in a society.
Ageism	Ageism refers to prejudice against a person on the grounds of age in the belief that the age category is inferior to other age categories and that unequal treatment is therefore justified.
Social status	Social status refers to a position in a social relationship, a characteristic that locates individuals in relation to other people and sets of role expectations.
Social stratification	The systematic, uneven distribution of valued products of social life such as wealth, power, and prestige among the occupants of different social statuses, is referred to as a social stratification.
Age Stratification	Age stratification refers to the inequalities, differences, segregation, or conflict between age groups.
Mode	In statistics, mode means the most frequent value assumed by a random variable, or occurring in a sampling of a random variable.
Social support	Social support is the physical and emotional comfort given to us by our family, friends, co-workers and others. It is knowing that we are part of a community of people who love and care for us, and value and think well of us.
Kinship	Kinship is the most basic principle of organizing individuals into social groups, roles, and categories. It was originally thought to be determined by biological descent, a view that was challenged by David M. Schneider in his work on Symbolic Kinship.

Cultural lag	The term cultural lag refers to the notion that society is unable to keep up with the rapid pace of technological change, and that social problems and conflicts are caused by this lag. It is also a Marxist principle, established as a way to describe the period after the proletariat revolution.
Industrial revolution	Industrial Revolution refers to the massive social, economic, and technological change in 18th and 19th century Great Britian. It commenced with the advent of the steam engine. Spread throughout Western Europe and North America in the 19th century.
Government	A government is a body that has the authority to make and the power to enforce laws within a civil, corporate, religious, academic, or other organization or group.
Industrial society	In sociology, industrial society refers to a society with a modern societal structure. Such a structure developed in the west in the period of time following the industrial revolution. They are generally mass societies,
Society	A society is a grouping of individuals, which is characterized by common interest and may have distinctive culture and institutions.
Authority	Authority refers to power that is attached to a position that others perceive as legitimate.
Community	Community refers to a group of people who share a common sense of identity and interact with one another on a sustained basis.
Community service	Community service refers to service that a person performs for the benefit of his or her local community. People become involved in community service for a range of reasons, for some, it is an altruistic act, for others it is a punishment.
Range	A measure of variability defined as the high score in a distribution minus the low score is referred to as a range.
Gerontology	Gerontology is the study of the elderly, and of the aging process itself.
Entitlement	The feeling that one has a right to certain privileges and that specific rewards should be forthcoming by virtue of what they have done or who they are is an entitlement.
Exploitation	In political economy, economics, and sociology, exploitation involves a persistent social relationship in which certain persons are being mistreated or unfairly used for the benefit of others. This corresponds to one ethical conception of exploitation, that is, the treatment of human beings as mere means to an end — or as mere "objects".
Elder abuse	Elder abuse refers to a term used to describe physical abuse, psychological abuse, financial exploitation, and medical abuse or neglect of people age 65 or older.
Sector	Sector refers to parts of the economy as judged by the economic activity that they constitute. For example agriculture, forestry, fishing and mining constitute the primary sector.
Organization	In sociology organization is understood as planned, coordinated and purposeful action of human beings to construct or compile a common tangible or intangible product or service.
Poverty line	The poverty threshold, or poverty line, is the level of income below which one cannot afford to purchase all the resources one requires to live. Thus, by definition, nobody lives below the poverty line.
Mean	In statistics, mean has two related meanings: a)the average in ordinary English, which is also called the arithmetic mean (and is distinguished from the geometric mean or harmonic mean). The average is also called sample mean. b)the expected value of a random variable, which is also called the population mean.
Preventive	Generally speaking, preventive medicine is that part of medicine engaged with preventing

medicine	disease rather than curing it. It can be contrasted not only with curative medicine, but also with public health methods which work at the level of population health rather than individual health.
Battery	In many common law jurisdictions, the crime of battery involves an injury or other contact upon the person of another in a manner likely to cause bodily harm.
Attitude	Attitude refers to an enduring mental representation of a person, place, or thing that evokes an emotional response and related behavior.
Conflict perspective	A theoretical perspective that focuses on the struggle among different social groups over scarce resources is referred to as conflict perspective or conflict theory.
Social status	Social status refers to a position in a social relationship, a characteristic that locates individuals in relation to other people and sets of role expectations.
Extended family	Extended family refers to a family group consisting of more than two generations of the same kinship line living either within the same household or, more usually in the west, very close to one another.
Social movement	A social movement refers to large informal groupings of individuals and/or organizations focused on specific political or social issues, in other words, on carrying out, resisting or undoing a social change.
Social change	Social change refers to alteration in social structures or culture over time.
Ageism	Ageism refers to prejudice against a person on the grounds of age in the belief that the age category is inferior to other age categories and that unequal treatment is therefore justified.
Social problem	A social condition that is perceived as having harmful effects is a social problem. Opinions about whether a condition is a social problem vary among groups and depend upon how and by whom the condition is defined and perceived in society.

Gerontology	Gerontology is the study of the elderly, and of the aging process itself.
Secularization	Secularization is a process of transformation as a society slowly migrates from close identification with the local institutions of religion to a more clearly separated relationship.
Society	A society is a grouping of individuals, which is characterized by common interest and may have distinctive culture and institutions.
Religiosity	Religiosity refers to a sociological concept referring to the importance of religion in individuals lives.
Community	Community refers to a group of people who share a common sense of identity and interact with one another on a sustained basis.
Attitude	Attitude refers to an enduring mental representation of a person, place, or thing that evokes an emotional response and related behavior.
Cohort	A cohort is a group of subjects, most often humans from a given population, defined by experiencing an event (typically birth) in a particular time span.
Empirical study	An empirical study in social sciences is when the research ends are based on evidence and not just theory. This is done to comply with the scientific method that asserts the objective discovery of knowledge based on verifiable facts of evidence.
Minority group	A minority group or subordinate group is a sociological group that does not constitute a politically dominant plurality of the total population of a given society.
Organization	In sociology organization is understood as planned, coordinated and purposeful action of human beings to construct or compile a common tangible or intangible product or service.
Social interaction	Social interaction is a dynamic, changing sequence of social actions between individuals (or groups) who modify their actions and reactions due to the actions by their interaction partner(s). In other words they are events in which people attach meaning to a situation, interpret what others are meaning, and respond accordingly.
Social isolation	A type of loneliness that occurs when a person lacks a sense of integrated involvement. Being deprived of participation in a group or community involving companionship, shared interests, organized activities, and meaningful roles causes a person to feel is a social isolation.
Social network	A social network is a social structure made of nodes which are generally individuals or organizations. It indicates the ways in which they are connected through various social familiarities ranging from casual acquaintance to close familial bonds.
Positive relationship	A statistical relationship in which high scores on one variable are related to high scores on another variable, is referred to as a direct or positive relationship.
Control variable	A variable introduced into a statistical analysis to see if a statistical relationship holds among people who are alike on a particular characteristic is referred to as a control variable.
Variable	A characteristic that varies in value or magnitude along which an object, individual or group may be categorized, such as income or age, is referred to as a variable.
Sect	A religious group that draws most members by persuasion from the lower class, that has an informal structure and an untrained clergy, is governed with minimal authority, has few formal rituals, involves spontaneous displays of emotion, and generally opposes the dominant institutions of its society is a sect.
Cult	In religion and sociology, a cult is a cohesive group of people (sometimes a relatively small and recently founded religious movement, sometimes numbering in the hundreds of thousands)

	devoted to beliefs or practices that the surrounding culture or society considers to be far outside the mainstream, sometimes reaching the point of a taboo.
Hierarchy	A hierarchy is a system of ranking and organizing things or people, where each element of the system (except for the top element) is subordinate to a single other element. A hierarchy can link entities either directly or indirectly, and either vertically or horizontally. The only direct links in a hierarchy are to one's immediate superior, or to one of one's subordinates.
Mean	In statistics, mean has two related meanings: a)the average in ordinary English, which is also called the arithmetic mean (and is distinguished from the geometric mean or harmonic mean). The average is also called sample mean. b)the expected value of a random variable, which is also called the population mean.
Bias	A bias is a prejudice in a general or specific sense, usually in the sense for having a preference to one particular point of view or ideological perspective.
Longitudinal study	A type of developmental study in which the same group of participants is followed and measured at different ages is a longitudinal study.
Range	A measure of variability defined as the high score in a distribution minus the low score is referred to as a range.
Taylor	Taylor was an American engineer who sought to improve industrial efficiency. He was one of the intellectual leaders of the Efficiency Movement and his ideas, broadly conceived, were highly influential in the Progressive Era. During the latter part of his career he was a management consultant, and he is sometimes called "The Father of Scientific Management."
Gender	Gender refers to socially defined behavior regarded as appropriate for the members of each
Psychotherapy	Psychotherapy refers to a systematic interaction between a therapist and a client that brings psychological principles to bear on influencing the client's thoughts, feelings, or behavior to help that client overcome abnormal behavior or adjust to problems in living.
Social forces	Social forces are the typical basic drives, or motives, which lead to the fundamental types of association and group relationship.
Durkheim	Durkheim sought to create one of the first scientific approaches to social phenomena. Along with Herbert Spencer, Durkheim was one of the first people to explain the existence and quality of different parts of a society by reference to what function they served in keeping the society healthy and balanced—a position that would come to be known as functionalism.
Disability	A physical or health condition that stigmatizes or causes discrimination, is referred to as a disability.
Consciousness	The awareness of the senzations, thoughts, and feelings being experienced at a given moment is referred to as consciousness.
Social change	Social change refers to alteration in social structures or culture over time.

Variable	A characteristic that varies in value or magnitude along which an object, individual or group may be categorized, such as income or age, is referred to as a variable.
Gerontology	Gerontology is the study of the elderly, and of the aging process itself.
Range	A measure of variability defined as the high score in a distribution minus the low score is referred to as a range.
Government	A government is a body that has the authority to make and the power to enforce laws within a civil, corporate, religious, academic, or other organization or group.
Developmental theories	Those that assert that personal characteristics guide human development and influence behavioral choices but that these choices may change over the life course are called developmental theories.
Depression	In the field of psychiatry, the word depression can also have this meaning of low mood but more specifically refers to a mental illness when it has reached a severity and duration to warrant a diagnosis, whether there is an obvious situational cause or not.
Mean	In statistics, mean has two related meanings: a)the average in ordinary English, which is also called the arithmetic mean (and is distinguished from the geometric mean or harmonic mean). The average is also called sample mean. b)the expected value of a random variable, which is also called the population mean.
Community	Community refers to a group of people who share a common sense of identity and interact with one another on a sustained basis.
Developmental process	Developmental process refers to at different stages of the life course a variety of factors can influence behavior; factors influential at one stage of life may not be significant at a later stage.
Society	A society is a grouping of individuals, which is characterized by common interest and may have distinctive culture and institutions.
Norm	In sociology, a norm, or social norm, is a rule that is socially enforced. Social sanctioning is what distinguishes norms from other cultural products such as meaning and values.
Symbolic interaction	Symbolic interaction refers to the use of symbols by people to present themselves to others and interpret one another's behavior.
Age Stratification	Age stratification refers to the inequalities, differences, segregation, or conflict between age groups.
Attitude	Attitude refers to an enduring mental representation of a person, place, or thing that evokes an emotional response and related behavior.
Significant other	Significant other is a gender-blind, politically correct term to refer to a person's partner in an intimate relationship without disclosing or presuming anything about his or her marital status or sexual orientation.
Reference group	Individuals almost universally have a bond toward a Reference Group. These are groups to which the individual does not have real membership, but to which he conceptually relates him/herself, and from which he might accept goals and values as a part of his/her self identity.
Social group	A group that consists of two or more people who interact frequently and share a common identity and a feeling of interdependence, is referred to as a social group.
Bias	A bias is a prejudice in a general or specific sense, usually in the sense for having a preference to one particular point of view or ideological perspective.
Longitudinal	A type of developmental study in which the same group of participants is followed and

study measured at different ages is a longitudinal study.

Cohort A cohort is a group of subjects, most often humans from a given population, defined by experiencing an event (typically birth) in a particular time span.

Life expectancy The number of years a newborn in a particular society can expect to live is referred to as a life expectancy.

Preventive medicine Generally speaking, preventive medicine is that part of medicine engaged with preventing disease rather than curing it. It can be contrasted not only with curative medicine, but also with public health methods which work at the level of population health rather than individual health.

Alcoholism Alcoholism refers to a disorder that involves long-term, repeated, uncontrolled, compulsive, and excessive use of alcoholic beverages and that impairs the drinker's health, work and social relationships.

Neighborhood A neighborhood is a geographically localized community located within a larger city, town or suburb. Traditionally, a neighborhood is small enough that the neighbors are all able to know each other.

Hospice A health care facility designed to counsel and care for the terminally ill is a hospice.

Institutiona-ization The term institutionalization is widely used in social theory to denote the process of making something (for example a concept, a social role, particular values and norms, or modes of behavior) become embedded within an organization, social system, or society as an established custom or norm within that system.

Poverty line The poverty threshold, or poverty line, is the level of income below which one cannot afford to purchase all the resources one requires to live. Thus, by definition, nobody lives below the poverty line.

Cohabitation Cohabitation refers to living together in a sexual relationship of some permanence without being legally married.

Divorce rate The number of divorces over a specified period per specified popularion.The divorce rate is often calculated per 1,000 population or by estimating the proportion of all marriages that are expected to end in divorce.

Tolerance Tolerance is a recent political term used within debates in areas of social, cultural and religious context, as an emphatic antithesis to discrimination, as such may advocate persecution. Its usage came about as a more widely acceptable alternative to "acceptance", the usage of which had been widely derided, as certain cases would not be considered by common society as acceptable.

Census A census is the process of obtaining information about every member of a population. It can be contrasted with sampling in which information is only obtained from a subset of a population. As such it is a method used for accumulating statistical data, and it is also vital to democracy.

Sex ratio Sex ratio is the ratio of males to females in a population. The primary sex ratio is the ratio at the time of conception, secondary sex ratio is the ratio at time of birth. In humans the secondary sex ratio is commonly assumed to be 105 boys to 100 girls. In human societies, however, sex ratios at birth or among infants may be considerably skewed by sex-selective abortion and infanticide.

Division of labor Division of labor is the specialisation of cooperative labor in specific, circumscribed tasks and roles, intended to increase efficiency of output.

Migration The movement of people from one country or region to another in order to settle permanently,

	is referred to as a migration.
Inner city	The areas composing the central neighborhoods of industrial cities which are subject to dilapidation and decay, with the more affluent residents having moved to outlying area is an inner city.
Crime rate	Crime rate is a measure of the rate of occurrence of crimes committed in a given area and time. Most commonly, crime rate is given as the number of crimes committed among a given number of persons.
Crime	Crime refers to any action that violates criminal laws established by political authority. A crime in a nontechnical sense is an act that violates a very important political or moral command.
Technology	The application of logic, reason and knowledge to the problems of exploiting raw materials from the environment, is referred to as a technology.
Elite	The elite is a relatively small dominant group within a larger society, which enjoys a privileged status which is upheld by individuals of lower social status within the structure of a group.
Interdependence	Interdependence is a dynamic of being mutually responsible to and sharing a common set of principles with others. This concept differs dinstinctly from "dependence" in that an interdependent relationship implies that all participants are emotionally, economically, and/or morally "independent."
Interpersonal relationship	An interpersonal relationship is a social association, connection, or affiliation between two or more people. They vary in differing levels of intimacy and sharing, implying the discovery or establishment of common ground, and may be centered around something(s) shared in common.
Median	The number that falls halfway in a range of numbers, or the score below which are half the scores and above which are the other half is a median.
Discrimination	Discrimination refers to the denial of equal access to social resources to people on the basis of their group membership.
Authority	Authority refers to power that is attached to a position that others perceive as legitimate.
Euthanasia	The act of painlessly ending the lives of persons who are suffering from incurable diseases or severe disabilities, sometimes called mercy killing, is referred to as euthanasia.
Interest group	Interest group refers to an organization that attempts to affect political decisions by supporting candidates sympathetic to their interests and by influencing those already in positions of authority.
Mass society	Mass society is a society in which the concerns of the majority – the lower and middle social classes – play a prominent role, characterized by extension of voting rights, an improved standard of living for the lower classes and mass education.
Family life cycle	The phases, or stages, of the family life span, each of which is characterized by changes in family structure, composition, and functions, is referred to as a family life cycle.
Social change	Social change refers to alteration in social structures or culture over time.
Organization	In sociology organization is understood as planned, coordinated and purposeful action of human beings to construct or compile a common tangible or intangible product or service.

CPSIA information can be obtained at www.ICGtesting.com
Printed in the USA
LVOW091609080113

314658LV00010B/28/A

9 781428 818200